Praise for

# THE EXPERIMENTALIST

"Tracey Armstrong has done it again with *The Experimentalist.* Pushing limits on wealth creation and working to scale our business platforms in multiple cities needs fresh perspectives, creative thinking, and courage. The Experimentalist breathes life on lives and organizations that are stuck in between the current and the future they see. Tracey is one of the most trusted coaching voices in my life and the lives of those we are developing."

**Colin Higginbottom**
**CEO, President – Sustainable Legacy Group**

"The principles and strategies revealed in this book can launch you to a whole new level of thinking and living."

**Dr Bob Harrison**
**"America's Increase Authority"**

"With his relentless study and personal experience, Tracey Armstrong will inspire you to shatter the boundaries of fear, past failure, and limitations to experience a new level of creative success in your life and business. If you're ready to take the next step in your life, career, and dreams, this book is the breakthrough you have been waiting for!"

**Joel Luce, Chief Executive Officer**
**Bridgecom Communications and Previon Health**

This book is for everyone who desires to push beyond their limits and reveal their greatness! This profound and powerful tool will allow you to unlock personal excellence by shifting the directions you think, restoring the ability to dream, and bringing to life unused courage and commitment. Tracey's passion will inspire you to take charge of results you produce, while making a meaningful difference in the lives of others.

**Rex Crain**
**Speaker, Author**

the EXPERIMENTALIST
the POWER to IGNORE LIMITS
TRACEY ARMSTRONG

ZEBULUN

Published by
Zebulun Publishing

To contact the author about speaking at your conference or church, please go to www.traceyarmstrong.com



ISBN: 978-1-949709-45-2 (Hardcover)
eISBN: 978-1-949709-66-7 (eBook)

# CONTENTS

Chapter 1

# THE EXPERIMENTALIST

When I was young, about seven or eight years old, I was an avid TV watcher. I spent a lot of time at home alone. With my personality, a thinking introvert, I really enjoyed being alone at home watching TV.

My favorite shows to watch were *The Three Stooges, The Little Rascals, I Love Lucy, Beretta, Columbo,* and *Cojack,* which I could not watch with my stepfather (a little mature for my age). The list doesn't stop there. I also liked *Tom and Jerry, Popeye, The Hulk,* and *Kung Fu,* with David Carradine. I know, what a lineup! Each program gave me a certain feeling!

Some made me feel as if there was a reason for my naughty side, that there was a purpose for my little naughty side. Lucy's naughty side gave her creative ideas and good schemes. The same is true for the Three Stooges and the Little Rascals.

Yet, I also wanted justice to prevail. I loved shows where the detectives always got their guy. Cops and robbers and cowboys and Indians were always welcomed. I really, really liked *Starsky and Hutch.* If you are from a country outside of America, you will not know most of these shows. Cops and robbers shows—we now call them murder-mysteries.

My stepfather, "Champ" was his nickname, introduced me to cops and robbers programs, which is interesting because we were not on the cops side of things. I would watch war movies and cowboys and Indians with my grandfather. My grandfather was a veteran.

It was all so much fun! Yet, the show that really got me going was *Kung Fu*! He was wonderful. He found himself drifting from one city to another where he ultimately had to help someone in some way. The thing that really got me, beside the Kung Fu scenes, was how he would go into a flashback and would gain information from his past that would give him wisdom for the moment. Every future problem was already solved from past experiences. I realized the power of pulling useful information from your past, painful or pleasurable experiences, to help you achieve goals or solve a problem.

I recently read a quote by Winston Churchill that brought me back to this thought:

> *I felt as if I were walking with destiny, and that all my past life had been but a preparation for this hour and for this trial . . . I thought I knew a good deal about it all, I was sure I should not fail.*

Winston Churchill created in my mind a new thought with that quote when he said, "I felt like I was walking with destiny" rather than saying "I felt like I was walking in my destiny." Winston Churchill's quote personified destiny rather than making it a simple destination bound in fate; that somehow destiny walks with you to make sure that everything you go through has a meaning and a reason to be; that somehow destiny is training you and me for the big event by making sure that we have in our arsenal the tools and weaponry needed for the task that is soon coming. Destiny is like Mr. Miyagi from *The Karate Kid*, training you for the big fight through everyday challenges—challenges that are destined by destiny to make you fit.

I realize that destiny has been training me and walking with me from my youth to write this book. Destiny has been preparing me for an event in a time that was still yet to come. Destiny is playing the infinite game and I was playing a finite game. I was living in my destiny each day rather than walking with destiny as my coach in life. Destiny has been making me fit for the journey ahead and the moment that reveals that I am ready for the assignment of my life.

Winston Churchill's life of success and failure all prepared him for one of history's greatest challenges—a challenge that many didn't recognize. Even if they did recognize the challenge, they didn't have a plan to deal with it. I recognized Winston Churchill was an alchemist because he not only recognized the need to act but was able to mix a solution from his past experience and future expectation. The cure was found amongst the ingredients of his life.

This is what an alchemist obsession is: one who searches for a solution using what is available. They believe that they can create a cure for the issue at hand from their everyday findings.

Winston was groomed by destiny to handle Hitler and the Nazi rise. From his early intrigue with war to writing about his exploits as a young soldier—this was all preparation that would eventually work for his benefit. There is not just one thing that made him right for the task; it was everything that he experienced in life that made him right for the job. It's not possible for me to pinpoint the successes and failures of Winston Churchill because the purpose of my writing *The Experimentalist* is not directly about Winston as much as his character is a perfect prototype of an alchemist/experimentalist—one that had been prepared through the journey for the challenge to be revealed. Whether you are on the journey or looking at the assignment, one thing is guaranteed: destiny has been preparing you for this moment.

Your experimentalist is about to be revealed. Your inventor is rising to the surface. Our current industry has hit such a stride toward achievement that we have locked into predictable success. This is great for the challenges of the past, but the challenges of the future need a kind of alchemy. It needs experimentation for the true solutions to be revealed. This is a kind of success that only comes through trying something new, where the only reference available is the chain link of experiences from your past that gives you the needed boldness and courage for experimentation.

Winston Churchill had never met a Hitler type before. Nor had he ever been called on to stand against such a world-changing challenge. Yet, what he had discovered about himself through the past is that he knew how to win and how to lose and how to make it all work for himself. Failure was no longer a concern, and winning was the only possible outcome.

As a young man, Winston learned to make the most of every opportunity. While he was on the battlefield, he wrote periodicals and became known as a writer who was also a soldier. This would be useful for him in the future just as it was useful to him then.

On the battlefield is where Winston Churchill began to unveil himself as a writer. It's like battle and writing were the perfect chemistry to inspire his thoughts. On the frontlines in India, he wrote a daily article for *The London Telegraph* known as "Frontier Letters," which later became his first book, *Mellencamp Field Force.* On the Sudan frontline, he wrote articles for *The Morning Post* that later became his second book, *The River War.* In 1899 he entered politics and lost. Then he returned to battle. During the Boer War, he was captured and spent his twenty-fifth birthday as a prisoner of war. He escaped from prison. He tried his hand at politics again in 1901 by running for Parliament and won.

The more I look into the life of Winston Churchill, the more I am encouraged by the many things that he was willing to try. It seems that he experienced nearly as many defeats as he did victories. The lesson that I have gathered from this is that he was unwilling to allow defeat or failure to keep him from experimenting. He tried everything that his imagination could hold. He tried painting and became an artist. He tried his hand at masonry and built a brick wall in his backyard. It was not the most successful attempt, so a companion of his corrected the flaws when Winston was away. Upon returning to the wall, he assessed his work and commented, "What a fine-looking wall!" He was willing to experiment and try new things.

This is the first step to being an alchemist: experimentation! Of course, we never let it be known that we are experimenting, but that is what it is.

## MASTER OF EXPERIMENTATION

Winston Churchill wrote himself into history by documenting events and circumstances of being on the battlefield. Through writing, he poised himself to be listened to in society. As a wordsmith, Winston separated himself from being a soldier to an author to a politician and to a statesman.

## MASTER OF EXAMINATION

Winston's writings were brilliant in examining the circumstances and relaying an explanation for events. The reader could easily come to a conclusion from his clear examination of the details.

This brings me to the next thing that I discovered about alchemy from Winston Churchill. An alchemist not only experiments, but he must also examine the result and explain the challenge and solution in order for it to become science or art.
Duplication is the product of examination and explanation. If the solution was not found, the examination and explanation will often reveal other possibilities.

After his time serving in the military, Winston Churchill pursued a career in politics. Following a season of success, he was removed from his political seat. In 1929 Winston Churchill was contracted to write *The Marlborough Life and Times*, the story of his ancestor who overcame King Louie the 14th. He had just lost office after spending twenty years in the cabinet. This gave him the free time to pursue this project.

His documentation of the historical account of his ancestor, John Churchill, prepared him for the greatest challenge of his century. His research revealed to him strategies and doctrines of a dictator. The more he researched, the more clearly he could recognize the profile. On one of his research trips to Germany, he saw the Nazi Reich in action. When he saw Hitler, he recognized the same spirit that was in Louie the 14th. He said that "Hitler loved war too much." Yet, it takes one to know one. Many thought that Winston loved war too much himself. His obsession with the war was different from that of Hitler's. Hitler loved war because he was obsessed with power. Winston was obsessed with it because he loved his Queen, country, and people.

He once scheduled a lunch with Hitler, but Hitler came to the door, looked, and saw Winston Churchill waiting. He turned and walked away, saying, "I don't need to meet with such a small man." Hitler underestimated the convictions of Winston Churchill. Churchill returned to England from his research tour with an exclamation: "Hitler is a dangerous threat!"

His exclamation was not immediately heeded by the world. During this time his four-volume, one-million-word historical documentation of John Churchill's story, *Marlborough,* was finished. It was a five-year work, from 1933-1938. This work sharpened him for the task ahead.

He was soon after elected as prime minister, for which many referred to him as "a wartime prime ministry." He was the right man for the job. This is when he spoke the quote that I used to open this chapter. Everything was working for him, and destiny was walking him into the very moment for which he was prepared.

Winston Churchill used his amazing oratory skills and writing prowess to move the resistance against Hitler and his Third Reich forward. Reports tell how Franklin D. Roosevelt was hesitant to get involved in the war with Hitler because the U.S. was dealing with Pearl Harbor and the battle with Japan. Winston sent FDR a leather-bound, personally signed copy of *Marlborough* with his special seal. A short time later Winston Churchill received a response of support from FDR. The U.S. was going to support Britain in the war.

This brings me to the fourth ingredient of alchemy that I discovered from Winston Churchill; the power of an exclamation. His outcry against Hitler was heard and read and hearts were moved to action.

The experimentalist consists of these four postures: (1) a willingness to experiment; (2) fearlessness of failure, and a greater fear of not trying; (3) a keen mind to examine the results, making sure that there is no room for improvement; and (4) the ability to explain one's findings and why they work in such a way that it changes the rules forever; it is necessary that whoever follows the explanation can receive the same results.

The result should generate a herald-like passion so that people can't help but talk about the findings.

Destiny has prepared each of us for this kind of alchemy. You and I are guided in this life. We simply need to be able to recognize the moment for which we have been prepared. This only comes to those who are accustomed to trying and failing until they find that trying something new and fresh is what they are made for.

Pain is a sign that we are alive. Instead of trying to make sense of the pain, an alchemist uses the pain until it makes sense. Thomas Edison said, "To invent, all you need is an imagination and a pile of junk." This is the second premise of this book: realizing that connected to the pain is a pile of junk, stuff that we deem useless. Yet, with a heart to invent and an imagination, you can make sense of your pain. You can make it something beautiful.

Destiny deals with how everything ends, in the end, the end of days. Destiny is not as concerned with how you feel in the process as with how you end. The process makes you the person necessary for the moment. There is a moment that you are being prepared for. The only way to recognize the moment is to keep preparing for it. Don't stop living for that moment because you have experienced pain. Under the pain is the junk pile where you will find the parts necessary for the moment.

The experimentalist is an inventor. They are looking to create something that has never been. They are driven to cure the problems and ills around them, whether that is in a corporate office, an impoverished country, in their home, or community. An experimentalist will never be satisfied with mediocrity. They must conjure. They must mix things up looking for a solution. They are solution- oriented. They have within them the three personalities: the maker, the breaker, and the master.

This is the journey that you are on. I hope to join you on this journey and inspire you to let the alchemist in you come to the surface. If you and I fully commit to this, we can see something amazing take place in the world. We can see a new revolution in the earth: the experimentalist revolution—a company of people who are not afraid to shoot for the stars and mix up our past and present to make a new future. We often wait for others to fix the problems, but maybe you are the solution. There is only one way to know: get started experimenting! Let the maker come out and play. Do something that makes a difference.

*The Experimentalist* is based upon the premise from these two quotes; One from Winston Churchill and the second from Thomas Jefferson who said, "To invent, you need a good imagination and a pile of junk." In short, destiny has and is preparing you to turn a junk pile into an invention. This is the moment that you have been born for. This is your moment! Join the revolution!

## Chapter 2

# WINGS OF AN EGO

In mythology, there is a story of extreme forms of the ego. Hubris and false humility are both extreme ends of an ego. These extremes are when someone is not congruent to their internal personhood, therein creating a conflict that must be masked. Because of the concern and fear of these trenches of ego, most people choose to believe that they do not need to possess an ego—unwittingly missing the understanding that their ego gets them out of bed each day and causes them to brush their teeth and get dressed. Those are the least demands that an ego presses upon a person.

Ego is what keeps you from giving up when there is still an opportunity to win. It's the grit in the teeth of a person who has been beaten yet pulls herself up one more time to give it another try.

You have one ego. You should let it out to play. I want to help you develop it and use it. But first, we must clear up a misnomer.

As I researched the ego, I found that psychology, sociology, and religions have been trying to either explain the ego or kill the ego. In my research, I found that the ego is something that people try to measure. Based upon the measurement, this determines its usable validity. For example: a person with a *big* ego is seen to be self-absorbed. They are labeled as egotistical and prideful. A person with a strong ego is self-confident yet aware of others. Measurable terms like "big," "small," "strong," "weak," or "super" are used to describe a person's "self" and their interaction with their surroundings.

Freud believed that the ego was a negotiation between human impulse and social norms. Based upon this thought process, your inner voice helps you make decisions using your human nature and what you believe people would accept as normal. If this is true, then I could improve my ego. I could change my nature. I could change my social standards. I just need to change my social environment.

We have all either seen or experienced this kind of development, whether it was graduating from junior high school to high school or from one job to another. Our ego helps us fit in or stand out. Depending on what our goal is, we are very adaptable if we choose to be.

As we look at the story of Icarus and his father, we see a story of how ego is susceptible to both of these factors.

I first heard the story from my son Yosef, as my wife and I were discussing the power of choice at the dining table. I had never heard of the mythological story Icarus. A few days later I heard another reference from Seth Godin. Seth is a world-renowned blogger and author. It sparked my interest. So I looked into the story.

The short version of the story is that Daedalus created a labyrinth for King Minor. King Minor wanted to imprison the Minotaur (a half-bull, half-human creature) in the labyrinth. The king used the labyrinth to torture and kill his enemies by putting them in with the Minotaur.

The king also imprisoned Daedalus and Icarus in a tower labyrinth. I found a couple of different versions that explain why they were now the king's prisoners rather than his trusted artisans. Yet, the reason for their imprisonment doesn't actually strengthen the moral of the story and is not needed to come to the conclusion. In the end,

Daedalus and Icarus are condemned to live their lives confined in the labyrinth.

Daedalus, Icarus's father, was a master craftsman. He was gifted with observation. One day Daedalus noticed that birds could come and go as they willed. He began to scheme a plan that would get them both free from the labyrinth. He planned to make wings that would carry them out of the labyrinth just like the birds. He collected feathers that the birds left on the ledge as they flew away. He also collected wax from candles as an adhesive. He then built a wooden harness-system frame, like wings. He meticulously placed feathers on the wing structure, holding them in place with wax.

Once both pairs of wings were finished, Daedalus informed Icarus of their escape plan. He instructed that once they were flying not to fly too low because they would be flying over the ocean and the sea water would soak the feathers, causing the wings to be too heavy to fly. This would cause them to fall into the ocean and drown. He then said to not fly too high. The higher they flew, the closer they would fly to the sun. The heat of the sun would melt the wax, causing them to lose feathers and fall to their deaths.

Icarus, fully sure of the instructions, launched out and left the labyrinth prison. To his amazement, he successfully flew. As the people on the ground saw them flying, they yelled, "The gods are flying!" Icarus was so encouraged by their praise that it motivated him to fly higher. The higher he flew, the greater the praise. Icarus was so enthralled with the praise of the people that he completely forgot the warning of his father.

It happened just as his father said that it would. The higher he climbed, the closer he came to the sun and the hotter the temperature became. One by one, Icarus's wings lost feathers. Icarus's ego was so stroked by the praise of people that he forgot who he was and what he was doing. His father could only watch as his son fell to his death.

This story teaches the difference between extreme hubris and extreme humility. The listener is to come to the conclusion not to stand out and not to be too humble. Just play it safe and stay in the middle. I believe that there is merit to playing it safe. Yet, sometimes, in order to achieve greatness, you must do something that is bigger than life.

It is socially acceptable to stay normal. There is one thing that makes a person rise from the norm: desperation! Icarus's and Daedalus's desperation caused them to be willing to do what others didn't. That is why there were only two people flying.

The crowd of watchers on the ground were many. Most people are content in watching others fly. The alchemist revolution is for the person who is on the ground watching and singing, "I believe I can fly. I believe I can touch the sky. I think about it every night and day. I spread my wings and fly away."

This is contrary to our upbringing. We start life with songs like "Jack and Jill went up the hill to fetch a pail of water. Jack fell down and broke his crown and Jill came tumbling down after." This song screams, "Don't go up the hill, Jack!"

If you go through the Rolodex of your life, you will remember many childhood development songs, poems, and stories that keep you grounded. We have been brainwashed with limitation from an early age.

In my book *Becoming a Pioneer of Success*, I shared research of how the triceps resist the bicep in a curl exercise when a limited mindset is present. The tricep pulls as the bicep pulls in the opposite direction, limiting the power and force available. The limiting mindset will sabotage potential before a person can get started. The reason for an action is just as important as the action.

Some time ago I received a news feed notification from CNBC. I followed the link and ended up reading an article on Khaled. Khaled is a hip-hop artist who performs the song "All I Do Is Win." The article featured a few of his tweets and a story of how he has been the financial provider for his family. His family story is a powerful immigration story of how his father moved to the U.S. with very little. The article said that Khaled's father only had $20 when they came to America.

Khaled remembers as a youngster helping his parents sell clothing from the family van. It was Khaled's twitter post that got my attention.

One of Khaled's texts impacted me in an interesting way. I didn't realize how my upbringing had set standards that limited my perspective. When I read the following tweet I had an interesting response.

> *I work every day. I have to. I have my family to take care of. My mom, my dad, and my whole fam depend on me so Ima go even harder!*

At first glance, I didn't know what bothered me. I know that what he was talking about was right. He was building something for his family. He felt the responsibility to make sure that they were taken care of, yet it was the personal pronouns used in the tweet. I had been thinking a lot about narcissism and the seeming self-importance found in this generation.

Then it hit me. The fact that I have been taught to say "we" instead of "me" was damaging to my confidence. Think about it! When I say "we" are going to do this or that, who is actually going to do it? I am! I was taught to say "we" when talking about something so that I didn't seem proud or arrogant. Yet, it was "me" that had the responsibility to get it done. I realized that we have a whole generation that has been displacing responsibility and hiding it behind "we." When I have to work harder, I can't put that responsibility on anyone else.

"I" is a word that clearly defines whose head should roll if the project doesn't work.

What "I" did! What "I" do! Can it be narcissistic if the person plans on being responsible and not simply entitled? Entitlement is a challenge because the person wants the rewards of a responsible person without accountability.

The best in the world, the top shelf, the one percenters want the responsibility. Their ego can handle it. Win or lose! They are the ones who say "give me the rock" when there are only seven seconds on the clock in the basketball game. Moments in life are created by people who have confidence just for that moment. They have an under-the-gun ego. They spend time dreaming about those moments.

If you take away the recognition from them, you take away their desire to do it.

In the scriptures, the apostle Paul writes, "I can do all things through Christ who strengthens me." He makes it clear that he can do whatever he is anointed by God to do. God has anointed you for a specific accomplishment. Yet, it will never happen until you bring your "I can" to the table. "I can" is the Greek word *ego.* Even God needs your ego. Your ego is important. If you remove "I can," you remove God from your life. This is the moment of a lifetime. We need you to bring your best to the game.

God needs your "I!" He needs your ego. It may seem strange to think that God rides on your ego. Success is not possible without your full engagement.

Everything that you think about, meditate on, and practice is what forms your ego. The things that you meditate on and practice mentally, emotionally, and intellectually all become fused to your soul and directly affect your ego. As you meditate, you change. As you mentally practice, you progress. The more you imagine, the more noticeable it will become to everyone who is watching you.

The more you repeatedly give your thoughts to a subject, the more you become committed to it. You will gradually move toward it, forcing it into view for all to see your progress. You should not seek to be unseen. Yet you should not seek to be seen. You should seek to make a difference. Then as you are seen, others will also believe that they too can make a difference.

The people who really get our attention are those who go all out. We are fascinated with people who are fascinating. Fascinating people are fascinated with something. This empowers their ego to achieve the impossible. Fascination removes apprehension. Fascination is not borrowed; it's personally owned. Fascination produces a level of ownership that cannot quit. It's what keeps you from quitting.

People who are surrendered to their passion are also surrendering their passion. There is a place where we are surrendered to a surrendered passion, meaning we have a feeling that what we are working toward is bigger than ourselves. Destiny is calling us to move ahead without hesitation. We surrender to the beckoning and nagging call. Deep is calling to deep and we are surrendering to it. In this surrendered place, we discover genius. Genius is found in surrendering to the call.

It's creation. What do I mean? Genius is not a collection of stored information. It's the ability to access the sixth sense—the very muscle that creativity uses to imagine and execute what has never been before. Genius and creativity are not separate functions. They are a collaboration between innovation and invention. Genius must create what they imagine to be true.

The idea of ego is completely misunderstood in our modern vernacular. A genius is a kind of ego. A genius must consider themselves to be a genius in order to discover the virtues of genius. Genius, according to Noah Webster in his 1828 dictionary, is "to beget, to procreate . . . to give birth as a father his son."

In ancient times it meant to live a guided life through the help of a spirit, a spirit that presides over a person's destiny. This may be where we got the idea of a guardian angel.

Many named geniuses believe that they were guided in their discoveries. We understand that genius has been described as a particular talent or aptitude. In all cases, a person must believe that they are capable of receiving, knowing, or discovering something that others look past. It is the very idea that Winston Churchill was walking with destiny that gave him the ego to address the world. The level of ego needed to say "I see Hitler and his Nazis as danger" when no one else believes this to be true is genius. Then once he handled Hitler, he began to warn the world about Stalin and the Russian iron curtain. Without a man with such an ego, history would have been different.

Winston Churchill birthed (beget) ideas into the mind of the world. He believed not only that he needed to, but also that he could. The power of "I can" is unstoppable.

Years ago I watched Oprah Winfrey interview Denzel Washington. I remember Oprah asking about pivotal moments in Denzel's life. He mentioned in his response a woman who attended his church when he was young. This woman told him that he would be an influential actor. (I am sharing this in my own words as I remember the interview.) He said that those words encouraged him as he grew in his career. Whether it's inspirational words from someone, an inward confidence, the still, small voice in your soul, or the yearning in your heart, they all help build and establish the necessary ego to become who you are destined to be.

I was also into football when I was a kid. I watched American football all the time. I had my favorites. I liked highlight reels. I liked to watch running backs break tackles and break away for a touchdown run. I would watch and imagine that it was me running for a touchdown. I found out that my friend was on a football team. I rode my bike to the practice field and asked the coach if I could join. I was just in time. The official season was about to start. I had one week to learn the plays. The coach immediately recognized that I was fast compared to my teammates and stuck me in the game. My position was halfback. I only knew one play: the halfback sweep!

On game day, the first play of the football game was halfback sweep. The quarterback pitched the ball to me and off I went. All I could think was, *Run as fast as you can!* Touchdown was my first play! It was amazing.

As I grew older I grew tall and skinny. I lacked the size of a halfback, my favorite position to play. This caused me to be apprehensive in my running. I was fast and had plenty of moves. Yet, I was not able to progress in the game because I couldn't pack on the weight. I ate stacks of pancakes and used supplements. None of those things gave me the confidence to run powerfully. My coach would tell me, "You are fast and have the moves but you lack intensity." Truth be told, I wanted to be a professional football player, but I lacked the ego to pursue it against all odds. I lacked the intensity because I lacked the necessary ego to achieve that dream. I liked it, but I didn't want it enough to take the hits. If you want something bad enough, you will take the hits as a part of the cost for it.

I soon dropped football and replaced it with dancing. I had always danced but never imagined that I could make money at it until one day I saw Michael Jackson do the moonwalk. When I saw him moonwalk, I decided then and there that I would be a dancer. We didn't have a VCR or YouTube at the time, so I had to practice from memory. Within a short period of time I was moonwalking around the house.

Then I heard of breakdancing. I became a breakdancing fool. I would carry vinyl flooring or cardboard everywhere. I was fascinated by dancing. Then one day someone saw me and my friends dancing and decided to be our manager. The next thing you know we were touring for Pepsi as the Pepsi breakers. I would run off stage at one point, change my costume, and reappear on stage as Michael Jackson and dance to "Billy Jean" featuring my moonwalking ability. I was doing what I could be intense about. I found what my ego was connected to: I was an entertainer.

I wasn't a football player. I liked when people cheered, but I didn't like the pain associated with the physical contact at 160-pounds soaking wet in high school. My favorite thing was to watch highlights of OJ Simpson, Billy "White Shoes" Johnson, Franco Harris, Walter Payton, and Earl Campbell. My ego only liked the entertainment aspect, not the pain.

When it came to dancing, I loved it all. When it came to acting, I loved it all. I could practice all day, every day. I was an entertainer. That's my thing.

God's grace was and is on me for entertaining—just like someone else has grace for hospitality and knows how to put on an incredible event and everyone looks forward to their events. There is grace for everyone. You have grace for something. Your grace will give you a strong, healthy ego in that area of your life. It will cause you not to have fear or shyness in that area. It could even come across as arrogant, but in actuality it's a graced ego. Of course, there is a counterbalance of servanthood and accountability to the people you serve with your grace, but you should understand that you are walking with destiny.

People with a strongly graced ego always have a sense of higher calling, a bigger inward yearning. When I was a kid, I used to think that I was living in a movie. I would ride my bike as if movie cameras were running. Some would call that narcissistic. I would suggest that it's a strong, healthy ego. It can become something unhealthy if a person becomes selfish and self-serving. If a person has been damaged and polluted by circumstance, then their healthy ego mixed with pain, fear of failure, or rejection can become self-exalting to cover their insecurity and inferiority.

When Winston Churchill was fired, he didn't pout; he didn't get bitter. His ego was healthy enough that he decided to do something different. He chose to become an artist. That's what a healthy ego can do. It can decide to grow and be beneficial in another way. It's a player who is too old to play and becomes an announcer or a coach. It's the model who is now older and has become a spokesperson for new products. A healthy ego will always find a way to continue to contribute to the world around them instead of insisting that the world change for them.

We can always find a new strength when we are faced with weakness. Where there is a weakness, there is grace to help you become strong and overcome limitations. If you notice a weakness in your life, realize that that weakness is being revealed to cause you to look deeper into yourself. Your walk with destiny will help you discover you. You will discover what you didn't know was there before the problem or weakness arose. If you can celebrate your weakness, it will illuminate your strengths. You will tap into the genius of you. You will receive divine help to become someone more than you are now.

Remember that genius means to beget. Often the genius ego is not revealed until an unfortunate circumstance forces it to be revealed—when something needs to be birthed.

The creative and life-giving portion of natural childbirth involves contractions, pushing, and pain. Restriction forces a contraction and prepares the cervix for birth. Not having experienced childbirth for myself, I can only understand from the many comments that come from a woman in birth pangs that it's painful.

So many great artists gave birth to their greatest creation through life's pain. Something awoke in them. For example, Horatio G. Spafford, the lyricist of "It Is Well with My Soul," experienced a horrible tragedy. He and his family survived the Great Chicago fires of 1871 but lost all of their real estate holdings to the fire.

In November 1873, the family planned a vacation to Europe. At the last minute, Horatio had to stay behind to handle some business. The vacation liner was struck and sank. Horatio lost his wife and four daughters in the accident. Later Horatio was sailing to Europe again. As the ship crossed the place where his wife and his daughters had drowned, the captain informed Horatio of the location. Immediately he sat down and wrote the hymn "It Is Well with My Soul" in a letter to his sister-in-law.

I heard it said that greatness is revealed when greatness is needed. I believe the same is true with creativity, artistry, and genius.

Most often genius is revealed only when called upon by circumstance.

As in the case of Horatio, the artist is often revealed through their challenge. Frustration or pain gives birth to the voice of an artistic genius.

What makes some people internalize and others externalize challenges? I would say that it has to be tied to a person's ego. A person's efficacy determines what meaning they will give to a circumstance. The more powerful a person feels, the more they feel they can handle the circumstance. If a person has confidence, then they can change or deal with circumstances that others would crumble under.

The more they feel empowered, the more confidence they have and the more likely they will make something of the challenge—whether it is sitting down and writing a hymn, like Horatio, or like in the case of Winston Churchill, who went home and built a wall, knowing that something would be revealed. A healthy ego will start doing something even if it's as simple as cleaning the house. This is bringing order to something chaotic and shows you that you have the power within you to still make change happen. Getting rid of external clutter also helps you create room and space in your thinking resulting in clarity of thought and creativity.

It's an ego thing. Instead of curling up on the couch, they choose to be productive with the energy of the moment. This works because creation is a soul issue. The soul is the host of your thoughts, feelings, emotions, and intentions. I am sure you, the reader, could add more attributes of the soul to this list. But let's just focus on this limited list for this ego portion of writing.

The soul is the throne of emotion. The more a person allows their soul to shine through, the more anointed and inspired they can be, meaning genius and creativity don't work halfheartedly. Creativity is a soul issue. Performers and artist do what they do from the soul.

Genius is a soul issue. It's when the unseen is able to press itself upon the mind, will, and emotions of a person who desires to see. The spirit of intelligence desires to cooperate with your intelligence and give you knowledge and wisdom of things not yet seen. The terms "knowledge" and "wisdom" clearly identify the faculty that you receive them by. Even though they come from the unseen and spiritual plain, they are brought into the seen through a soul. With that said, in order for you to be at your best, you must give your best to everything you do.

Humans are God's only creation that doesn't live to its full potential at all times. We don't live our full potential instinctively. We must choose to give our full heart, mind, soul, and will to a matter. For this reason, love is the only motivator.

Yet, love is not enough. Even if you love something or someone, you must choose to form the necessary actions in your mind, will, and emotion. Otherwise, you will find yourself loving on through your emotions and never calling upon the actions to prove your love.

Everything created has been given the power to excel. Whether you believe in God or some other origin, we all must agree that nature works hard to maximize its potential. A blade of grass grows every day to reach its allotted measure for that day. A tree is always reaching for more. Even if you take a house plant and move it away from the window, it will do its best to reach toward the light as it twists itself to stretch for new heights and new levels.

In my perspective, God has put in everything the potential to reach and grow beyond each day's limitation. We must believe in ourselves in order to cooperate with our given potential. In order to grow, we must equal our intensity to match our potential. Working with God's gifts and potential is like working with a workout partner.

Growth happens when you push yourself to the max. A good workout is to go to the point of failure. Continue until your muscle can no longer perform the exercise, at which point your workout partner kicks in and helps you finish the rep. A really good lifting partner, called a spotter, will also encourage you to go one further than the last rep with their help, forcing you to push beyond your limitation and move you into a growth mode.

Most people do not work out to the point of failure and they do not achieve the results that they desire. The same is true in life. Most people don't push themselves to achieve, but at the same time they expect an act of God to make the impossible happen.

The novel *The Help* was Kathryn Stockett's first novel. She began writing it after the September 11 attack on the World Trade Center. It took her five years to complete and the novel was rejected by 60 literary agents.

Many would have thrown in the towel after 30 rejections from literary agents. You must do it with all of your heart! Bring your ego to the game!

Let's take one more look at Paul the apostle's statement for a counterbalance to our healthy personal ego. He says, "I can do all things through Christ who strengthens me." I believe the key factor in having a healthy ego is to know the reason behind your ability. A second factor is knowing your personal limitations. Paul said that Christ's strength was his limit. In essence, Paul's ego needed to equal God's ability.

Winston Churchill was strengthened by the realization that destiny was walking with him to achieve the impossible. He had a healthy ego with an external source of strength and power. Remember that the ancient meaning of genius is to live a guided life by the assurance and help of a Spirit or divinity.

There is power and strength available for you to be a genius. Limitations will be removed when your ego matches your God potential. Which came first, your ability to create or God's desire to see you create? Do you create because you see it or is it because God wanted you to create it?

Like Icarus, do you fly because you are skilled or can you fly because God wants you to experience flying?

The goal is not to destroy your ego. I am trying to empower it! Release it! Your ego is the key to becoming strong like God and revealing your genius.

Your ego keeps you going when others quit. It's the power behind power statements that set your direction—absolute statements that burn the bridge toward defeat such as "I shall never surrender or retreat," declared by Lt. Col. William Barret Travis in his written address during the Alamo; or Winston Churchill's, "Never, never, never give up!" This resolve is only found in a persistent ego, in the mind and heart of a person who demands "victory at all cost"—also a Churchill quote.

We started this chapter talking about Icarus. Where did Icarus go wrong?

It was the meaning that Icarus gave to that moment that stole his strength. The meaning that he gave to it became the words and pictures that he gave to it, words and pictures that became the ego that he lived in. Or should I say died by? His ego was what I would describe as unhealthy. The way that people looked at him was important enough to cause him to adjust his ego, the way he saw himself.

When your ego can be moved by others' opinions, it is less than healthy.

Each achiever that we have studied had an internal compass that guided them. They all had an internal conversation built of pictures and words that guided their every decision. This can be something naturally innate. It could be because of their upbringing, even their personal self-talk. They could even be narcissistic. Either way, the pictures and words inside of them drove their beliefs, behaviors, and ultimately their deeds. This can be achieved intentionally by repeatedly feeding certain pictures and words to your subconscious.

Our internal voice is created and maintained by the words and pictures that we feed and hold in our minds. These words can be random and supplied by default or they can be intentional and based upon a certain design. If you grew up in a house where success was normal or achievement was a part of life, you will already possess a very proactive way of life and you will have many of these principles inherently within. Words and pictures that come from your family heritage help make up your ego. Oppositely, you may have experienced poverty, scarcity, and lack, and that picture created in your mind hatred for it. At which point any words and pictures that could be associated with poverty, scarcity, and lack can become a trigger point of some form of emotional energy—anger energy, which can be used to move you ahead, or shame energy, which can keep you stagnant.

I met a man from Nepal who was visiting the U.S. for the first time. He was dressed in new jeans, new leather shoes, and a new leather coat. He looked great! It would be hard to know that all his life he had been living in abject poverty. He had been in the U.S. for a few weeks and was already experiencing subtle changes, not only in his appearance but also in his emotions. I asked him what he thought of his experience in America. He said that he saw things over that last couple of weeks that he didn't know were available. His perspective had been changed simply by seeing the prosperity available in the U.S. He also mentioned that it could change his level of contentment going back to Nepal. It was something that he didn't know if he would want others in their village to experience because once they encountered the prosperity, how could they be satisfied with less?

New images and new words created a new picture within him. His ego was strengthened in the sense that he found that he could have things that he didn't know existed two weeks prior.

Whenever I want to take my team to another level, I introduce them to environments that will expand them. When the number-one hotel in Seattle was the Hotel 1000, I booked them all a night stay to experience the service and quality of the hotel. That experience alone launched our organization into its next level. I once flew them and their families to Disneyland for a few days with one assignment: talk to the crew and discover something about Disney that I didn't already know. Ride the rides, eat the food, enjoy the hotel but at the end of the day we would meet at a nice restaurant and talk about what we had learned and how to implement it in our organization. Again the organization grew. Why? Because we intentionally fed them new words and pictures, which in turn created new beliefs and behaviors that empowered them to achieve what they now owned internally. The ego of our organization changed. Things that once seemed hard didn't seem difficult any longer.

Icarus's father, Daedalus, should have spent more time giving his son a healthy ego before they took off. Self-confidence would have kept his son from giving in to the applause of the crowd.

Sometimes the greatest trap is that we don't know what to do after we have escaped the limitation. Once Icarus left the confines of the maze, he didn't have anything to keep him focused except for what not to do. He needed to have another goal. If you don't have another goal after achieving the goal to survive, you will fall—for the simple fact that your ego is destined to achieve, to have more than survival. If you don't give it a higher goal, it will drive you to sabotage so that you can start all over again. Don't let your ego's drive be developed by other people's acceptance of you. You are destined to achieve. You are made to fly. Fly with all your might.

Destiny is calling you to fly higher, not just to escape but to really live the way you are destined to live.

A healthy ego is a friend of uncompromising obsession. Live with passion—no, better yet, live in obsession.

## Chapter 3

# OBSESSION

Recently, I was invited to dinner with a new client. As we entered the restaurant, the Winter Olympics was on television. He asked me if I had been able to catch any of the Olympics. My immediate response was no, not really. I then remembered that a few days earlier I was in a hotel in Washington, DC, mesmerized for hours watching curling. I didn't correct my statement because curling isn't something that I would normally watch during the Winter Olympics. I almost felt a little embarrassed that it had occupied hours of my time.

Later that evening as I prepared for bed I went over my thoughts for the next morning's talk. My client had asked me to talk about obsession. As I went through my talk, I realized why I was mesmerized by curling. I grew up in a home with a two-time Olympic medalist. The only way that you can get into the Olympic games is by being obsessed with your sport. The Olympians that I met walk, talk, and think their sport every moment of the day.

I realized that the same would have to be true with curling. As I watched the U.S. women's team, they displayed absolute obsession and intensity about something that I knew nothing about. I watched every move. I listened to every scream, shout, and command, trying to figure out what they meant. The reason is that I am obsessed with people and why they do what they do. I try to figure it out all day. Just after I was glued to the screen watching curling, I fell into the same hole watching sumo wrestling. I also found myself watching bull riding. I love watching obsessed people do what they do. Their passion somehow goes beyond their personal experiences and challenges me to rise to greater heights.

Young children are very impressionable. My life choices have much to do with what I was exposed to as a child, the way I look at circumstances, the way I deal with people. My ambitions and my insecurities are a byproduct of how I processed the culture and environment of my childhood. My uncle was sent to a Boys and Girls Club as a child in order to keep him from falling into a gang or getting involved in drugs. His environment was an increasingly challenging and dangerous urban neighborhood. At the Boys and Girls Club, he met boxing coach Joe Cloud. My uncle was highly impressed with Joe. Joe Cloud became known for the boxers he produced. He produced Golden Glove champions and Olympians. Amongst them you would find names such as Sugar Ray Leonard and Leo Randolph.

My uncle was amid a tribe of champions in the making. The challenges of urban living continued to develop in Tacoma, Washington, to the point that Grandmother and Grandfather decided to move us to Puyallup, a rural area outside of Tacoma. I didn't have a tribe of champions like my uncle—well, except for those in my own house. Yet, they didn't want me to box. They always told me that it was not good for my brain. They said that I should use my brain.

I didn't know what to do with that statement until one day a mobile library came to our neighborhood. My friends and I ran into the truck. Each one of us picked out a book to read. I picked a book on the life of Howard Hughes. I chose it because I wanted to be rich. I knew poverty. I saw drinking, gambling, and abuse. I wanted to know what it was like to be rich. I wanted to be rich. I wanted to be a wealthy person. So I grabbed the only book that I could find on being rich and checked it out.

Reading that book on the life of Howard Hughes developed an appetite for a certain quality of life. Before reading that book I never heard of anyone having a movie theater in their home. From that point, I have dreamed of having a full-size theater in my home. Not just a few chairs or comfy sectional couch and a mediocre video projector—I am talking about a full-size screen, with loud full-surround, lots of chairs, and theater popcorn.

I needed to learn how to have that kind of life. From that moment I was intrigued with becoming successful. I wanted to understand what makes some people successful and others not—not just successful, but wealthy.

I was surrounded by success. My uncles were Golden Glove boxers and high-achieving athletes. I saw them work hard toward their goal every day. I lived with them while they were working to make weight for their next boxing match. I saw the discipline, but I didn't recognize it. I didn't recognize the daily work and sacrifice they put in to achieve what they hoped for. They were obsessed with sports and especially boxing. I was obsessed with TV, the action figure Stretch Armstrong, and money. I liked sports and was good at sports, but I didn't have the obsession to maintain absolute devotion toward its pursuit.

They were obsessed with boxing. I was obsessed with success.

Even though my uncles' paths and assignments were not the same as mine, the level of obsession was equal. Each of us had given ourselves to the desire. The yearning is the sign that it is possible. The price is the only thing that will need to be accepted.

I enjoyed sports, but I wasn't obsessed with it. My football coach said that I hesitated; I was apprehensive. His exact words were, "You are fast, but you lack intensity." Obsession is the level of intensity and passion necessary to stand out and lead the pack in whatever field you work within. Abraham Maslow, the father of psychology, said it this way: "A musician must make music, an artist must paint, a poet must write if he is to be ultimately at peace with himself."

Have you ever seen the face of someone who is focused and all in? We often call it being stone-faced or flint-faced. It means that someone's gaze and direction are so set that you can't break them.

The scriptures reveal that as Jesus was getting near the end of His assignment, He intensified His resolve. He steadfastly set His face to go to Jerusalem. He was so obsessed with getting to His destination, Jerusalem, that He didn't seem concerned with the Samaritans. The Samaritans rejected Jesus, as He may have appeared to be preoccupied with getting to His next destination.

It is much like when you are in an appointment with someone and they constantly look at their watch or phone to check the time. You can't help but think that they have somewhere more important to be. This causes you to hurry along or simply end the meeting.

Obsession makes you so focused that you seemingly look past everything and everyone that doesn't have anything to do with the object of obsession.

Obsession is a key factor in manifesting your full potential.

Obsession is not hereditary nor is it passed along like a disease. Obsession is a fixation, a fascination with something at such a level that it compels you and occupies your attention.

Obsession is a level of passion that will never allow you to be apprehensive. Apprehension is the most destructive force to your creativity. Apprehension suffocates a creative person, keeping them from truly discovering what they can bring into being. Apprehension is the enemy of someone who has the ability to make great things happen. Your ability to solve problems is contingent on your ability to tap into the creative force. Your passion must be equal to or greater than the issue in order to find a solution.

Obsession demands more of you than what you want to give. Yet, at the same time, you know that what is asked of you is necessary. Obsession makes you look past fear into the possibility. This activity brings your imagination to life.

Obsession works hand in hand with curiosity and creativity; without it, you will lack the necessary energy to master your craft, thus leaving you unable to solve problems in a professional way.

Hesitation is the enemy of obsession. I know that obsession as a word has a bad rap. But there is not another word that describes the kind of passion that you must have to solve your problems and reach your dreams.

Obsession is the only word that describes the kind of curiosity that must be possessed to achieve the extraordinary. People with obsession are not easily distracted from the task.

Obsession is a noun that means "the domination of one's thoughts or feelings by a persistent idea, image, desire, etc." It derives from the Latin word *obsessiōn*, which stems from *obsessiō*, meaning blockade, siege. Obsession blocks things out or blocks thing in. It's the process of surrounding thought and holding it in your mind until you find its source of power.

## LOCK ON, LOCK OUT

Have you ever looked for something for a long time? Once you find it you realize that you have been looking past it the whole time. My grandmother would often say, "It's right there. If it was a snake it would have bit you." What is that? It's the blockade principle of obsession. You start the search with a clear hope to find what you are looking for. After a few minutes, you tell yourself, *I am never going to find it.* At this point, the blockade principle starts to work with your mind to prevent you from seeing it until it's so obvious it could have bitten you.

When a person becomes obsessed and fixated with not finding something, they will not see it. This also works if you decide that you will find something. It will simply appear as if by magic.

Your ability to see is based upon what you are looking for—meaning, if you are looking for things to be difficult, then you will see the difficulty in things. It's that simple. The larger challenge is that when you have now locked in on a certain sight, it's harder to change what you see. Turning to see the other perspective is challenging.

This is often seen in a well-known example: using a drawing that has two perspective options. You might see an old woman, but with a quick adjustment of your perspective, you will see a young woman. It is often challenging to move back and forth between the two because your perspective is designed to lock onto one perspective and lock out the other. It is even more challenging, most likely impossible, to see both the young woman and the old woman at the same time. I don't know anyone who can see both, but I leave it open for someone to tell me that they can.

This is the blockade principle. It is absolutely necessary to achieve your dreams and goals. The more obsessed you are with an idea or goal, the more you will see how to make it happen. At the same time, this will cause you to see less of other things. Many people cannot get focused—I mean truly focused. The cause? They have not given themselves permission to obsess over their desires and dreams. Focus blocks out distractions and locks in on an idea or goal. This leads you to insights that are missed by those who approach the same goals or dreams with mediocrity.

Our brains are hardwired for this kind of focus. The Reticular Activating System in our brains is designed to help us block in or block out things that help us reach our goals. This is why goal-setting is not a suggestion; it is a necessary activity that must be used as a principle of life. You are hardwired to achieve goals. Your nervous system, subconscious, creative subconscious, and conscious mind will work toward and target whatever you give it. It will work while you are awake and as you sleep.

It's also called being flint-faced. When I first heard this term I didn't know what it meant until I was watching a survival reality TV program with my sons. The survivalist used a hard rock called a flint rock. This made me think of that statement. I had recognized that flint-face while growing up with world-class athletes. I called it their game face. It's the face of a person who is obsessed with winning. On the days that they had it, they won; and on the days when they didn't have it, they lost.

Game face and flint-faced are stern and hard-looking faces that show what's happening on the inside of a person. They have a resolute goal. Their meditation on winning gives them a focus that shows on their face. They are obsessed! They are focused. They have one thing on their mind and cannot be distracted. Winning is a must! Victory is the only plan.

When I am with someone who is flint-faced, it somehow gets me fired up also. Just like the flint rocks make sparks when two of the same interact and produce fire, so too this same effect happens when I am with someone with a dream that they are obsessed with. I too get all fired up about my dreams while talking with them, in the same way that iron sharpens iron.

When you spend time with people who are not obsessed with winning, achieving, and moving the organization to the next level, it is hard to keep the conversation moving. The spark slowly dies in you if this is the company that you keep. If you build a community around you that is obsessed with moving the ball down the court or moving the needle in the organization, there will be a fire in the camp and things will spark. Things will happen and things will get done. Every team needs sparky people, obsessed people. Don't hide the passion.

I recently heard that some corporations were going to tell their people to stop showing emotions on their face because it may make people from other countries feel uncomfortable. That is the most ignorant idea ever. The people who immigrate to the U.S. do so because something has been accomplished in a very short period of time. America is a world-leading, competitive nation because we have not hidden our emotions. We lead because we are obsessed with leading. We are not ashamed of emotion because emotions cause us to win. Win the lottery and show no emotion? Impossible! Win the office contest for a toaster and not show any emotions? Impossible! If you like the toaster, we will know; and if you don't eat toast, we will also know.

The winner circle is all about the emotion. If I live in an impoverished nation, winning separates me from poverty. We do business with a handshake and a smile. Take that away and our marketplace will look like everyone else's. A person with nothing can win in America because we want to see you smile and enjoy life. All are welcome if you can smile.

There is a scripture that connects a flint-faced life to a life without shame. Thus, we need to know that shame tries to keep us from being all in and obsessed with our dreams, gifts, goals, and desires. If you feel uncomfortable being all in and obsessed, ask yourself one question: "What am I ashamed of?"

Webster's defines "flint" as "a hard stone, used for striking fire, something very hard or unyielding." Being unyielding and unreasonable toward the dreams and goals that you have is the key to achieving them.

Seeing the end from the beginning is vital for obsession to exist. If you can't imagine what the victory looks like, you will never produce the level of heated passion necessary to make it to the end. Obsession always starts with what you see and then moves into a position of curiosity and onward to crafting it.

## THE THEORY OF THE MAKER'S OBSESSION

The more I study obsession, the clearer the equation becomes. Let me give you the equation: c2 + sc = P2—which breaks down to curiosity/creativity plus skillful craft equals performance/professionalism.

There are three ingredients that I have extrapolated from obsession. These three ingredients comprise the equation above. The first of the three is the maker's ingredient. The second is the breaker's ingredient. And the third is the producer's ingredient.

Before we dive into the equation, we should recognize that obsession is the force behind many of the things that we admire in people. We are intrigued by their lives and story. We read books about them and watch movies of their unequaled obsession to overcome obstacles and to win.

Albert Einstein was obsessed with the mysteries of the universe. Thomas Edison was obsessed with solving problems. Michelangelo was obsessed with the beauty of creation. Mother Teresa was obsessed with helping the poor. Winston Churchill was obsessed with the history of war. Jesus was obsessed with His Father's business. What was the source of their drive? I call it the maker's ingredient, which is curiosity and creativity.

Curiosity is what makes you look deeper into a certain subject. Creativity is what happens when you discover new insights based upon that curiosity. Curiosity/creativity is the first step.

You will focus on whatever grabs your curiosity. I assume that you have heard the old statement that curiosity killed the cat. I am not sure if curiosity has killed any cats, but the lack of curiosity would have killed humanity by now. Curiosity fostered the adventurous desire to search for land beyond what could be seen. Curiosity stimulates astronauts to test the limits of space. Without curiosity, there would be no discoveries.

Telling a child to stop being so curious is criminal. Our future depends on their curiosity and creativity. We need them to discover the cure for diseases that haven't been discovered yet. The concern of a parent, teacher, etc., is, what will happen if they become too curious or too obsessed? We all know that the words "obsession" or "obsessed" are used in a negative light. They give the imagery of a creeper stalking someone or of an over-possessive boyfriend or girlfriend. These are, of course, perverted perspectives of a very positive emotion. What most of society calls obsession is more like oppression. It goes without saying that obsession needs boundaries and oppression needs to be broken. Obsession is the very fuel needed to overcome oppression.

Starting with the maker's ingredient, the alchemist also sets boundaries and purpose to their obsession. They must possess a beneficial purpose beyond themselves for their obsession. Traditionally, kings and queens are anointed for their position. They received divine power to occupy and fulfill their position.

In the scripture, Jesus of Nazareth announced His mandate by reading a passage from Isaiah, stating, "The Spirit of the Lord is upon me to . . ." It is vitally important that you know what the Spirit of the Lord is upon you to do. The anointing teaches you, guides you, and instructs you. You must believe that your life is important enough to be guided by an eternal design, something bigger than yourself calling you higher.

Have you ever had a passion that seemed almost instinctive? A drive and desire that gripped you in a way that was different from any other? This is the draw of obsession. You are obsessed to fix something, try something, help someone or something. I have heard of doctors and nurses whose first patients were mice, rabbits, dogs, cats, or even birds. They worked to save these creatures when they were children. Their desire was associated with what the Spirit of the Lord was upon them to accomplish. They started practicing their mercy gift at a young age. They didn't have any medical training, but every injured animal, friend, or family member that would allow it would be a patient. This was something that was innate to them. It was in their heart before they read their first medical book.

It is the thing that your dreams are made of. It occupies your waking moments. This is your obsession. You must give yourself to your obsession while stabilizing it with proper boundaries.

The standards and boundaries you set for your obsession are one and the same—meaning, when you set a standard, that standard also sets what is not allowed. The standard and the boundary are the same.

Many are afraid to give themselves to the standards of their obsession, fearing that they will lose the balance. That's why you must set them both based upon what you are anointed to do.

Doctors are obsessed with their science, so they take a Hippocratic oath to save lives and not to take a life. They set both the standard of saving lives as well as the boundary never to take life. It's like a golf swing: one gives power to the other. The backswing is the power for the forward swing, which in turn gives the ball motion. What are you anointed for? It's the backswing to your obsession. The thing that you love is also associated with the very thing you hate. Don't be afraid of giving yourself to the obsession.

People are often concerned that their obsession will control them and lead them into some form of perversion. The difference between obsession and perversion is the why behind it. Again, I will ask the question, why are you anointed? Without a why, your desire is perverted. Obsession is the motor of creative genius.

Obsession should be associated with creative geniuses like Albert Einstein. He was driven to prove the theory of relativity. His creative genius was perverted by those who didn't possess his same values.

Einstein was a pacifist, yet his discovery of the theory of relativity was the science behind the nuclear atom bomb. It was not the reason for his obsession with the theory of relativity; but others who didn't share his passion, standards, or boundaries for this science changed the use and meaning of the discovery.

The maker's ingredient is C2 of the equation, which is curiosity and creativity.

## CURIOSITY AND CREATIVITY

Charles Dickens was so curious about humanity and creating characters that he walked the streets of London in the middle of the night for 20 miles to stimulate his creativity. He would notice the different and unique things about people and London city life as he walked. Many of his characters and scenarios were created during these walks.

The power of curiosity and creativity is key to starting the engine of obsession. If you are not curious, you will never be obsessed enough to engage the higher-level passions of the creation.

What captures your curiosity? What makes you look deeper? Discover this and focus all your energy toward it. Then you will have discovered the power of creativity.

At this point, the next ingredient will reveal itself. You will become obsessed with mastering the material needed to create your idea. This is when "the breaker" reveals itself. The breaker is the power to take raw material and turn it into something beautiful.

In order to execute your ideas, you will have to believe that you have the power to do so. You can only manipulate raw material into whatever you imagine when you believe that you are powerful enough to make change happen.

Thomas Edison turned ideas into experiences. Michelangelo turned marble into beautiful sculptures. There is a story in the scriptures that refers to when Jesus was on a boat with His followers. The boat was being hammered by the waves. They woke Him from His sleep and told Him of the peril that was about to take place. They even accused Him of not caring.

He woke from His sleep and told the storm to become peace. The seas calmed, and His followers wondered what kind of person has the power to control the sea and the storm. The answer? A person who understands that they have the power to control matter. This is the same power that the person who made the chair or couch that you are currently sitting on possessed. It was first an image in their imagination and then they found the raw material that would allow them to develop their idea into reality.

Another story in the scriptures tells of Jesus turning water into wine. The insight that we must gain from this is that the limitation is not the material but the imagination that is needed to see the material in a way that has never been seen before. If all you see is water, then you will never be able to make it wine. If all you see is a storm, then you will never be able to turn it into peace. If all you see is a huge chunk of marble, then you will never be able to chisel it into a beautiful statue.

If you imagine the raw aspect of a thing, then you will have the power to manipulate the raw material into something that no one else sees. Remember, all you need in order to be an inventor is an imagination and a pile of junk.

An inventor breaks the laws associated with one item in order to present it as something completely new, giving it a new meaning. This can be done with material, as in metal and rubber. People have the power to reinvent themselves and the world around them. I remember hearing of Robert Downey Jr.'s reinvention of himself years ago. He was wasting his life away with drugs and partying. I saw in the news that he trashed a hotel room while partying and was kicked out of the hotel. The rumor was that he was unemployable as an actor. What a terrible thing to be gifted and yet not able to be hired. When he returned to Hollywood as Tony Stark/Iron Man, it was epic. It has set him apart as one of Hollywood's great comebacks. I saw him in an interview in which he gave the credit for his reinvention to having a child.

Who knows what the alchemy will be for you to shift into your next level. But if you need to reinvent yourself, the motivation is found in the maker's ingredient.

The power of curiosity causes you to break rules, natural laws, and limitations. You will see a better and different way than what has already been discovered. This will start a creative process. I have worked with entrepreneurs who lost interest in a successful company only because they wanted to give themselves to creating another product or business. They were stirred by curiosity more than the already achieved success. Everything that is made started with someone's curiosity and creativity.

You are born to create. You have within you the power to change anything that you put your mind to change.

Mr. Goodyear, for example, changed what were the known uses of rubber. During his day, rubber was used for balls, shoes, tires, and a few other things, but there was a problem with it. It would lose integrity under extreme hot or cold temperatures. Any friction or heat would cause the rubber to become gummy. He spent much of his time experimenting with additives, hoping that something would solve the issue. He tried adding magnesium, but that didn't work. Then he made a concoction of white lead and sulfur and applied it to a piece of fabric. That didn't work either.

Frustrated, he left it and walked away. When he returned to his work area, he found that the fabric had somehow fallen onto a hot stove and was burning. As he grabbed it to throw the charred and burned piece in the trash, he discovered that the consistency had changed. He then realized that it would work to heat the new mixture as a part of the development process. That day history was made. The process is now called the vulcanization of rubber. This process is named after the mythological god of fire.

It is a mystery to me how that piece of fabric was placed on a stove. Some speculate that it was accidentally knocked off of the shelf onto the stove. No matter how it got there, the solution was discovered and Mr. Goodyear was able to rename the material. In giving it a new use, he gave a new meaning to the material, ultimately changing the name. Vulcanized rubber is commonplace today. Now it's something that most people use daily. It's on your car and your bike. It's found in your kitchen, as well as in your classrooms. It's all around you. We just call it rubber.

Before it was known as something different, rubber was gum from a plant that, when processed, changed the rules and made something new. Mr. Goodyear gave it a different meaning by giving it a different use and, in turn, broke a law and created another law of rubber. He changed the meaning and changed the name.

The process of creation changes the laws, changes the name, and changes the meaning.

This is not limited to the material world. If you change the meaning of something in your life, you change it forever. Change the experience by changing the story. Change the story by changing the expectation.

Your level of creativity depends on the meaning that you give to words such as "good," "unfortunate," and "challenging."

Manipulation of raw circumstances of life and raw material is determined by whether you call a circumstance usable or painful.

If you rename your current or past pain or problem as something you can change, then you will be able to make it something amazing.

Michelangelo was a world-renowned artist. He is known for painting the ceiling of the Sistine Chapel in the Apostolic Palace. It is said that painting wasn't his premier skill. His greatest works are recognized in sculpture. His famous sculpture of David is one of the most notable of his works. Michelangelo had a challenging life from before birth.

When Michelangelo's mother was three months pregnant with him, she fell off of a horse. Her injuries left her unable to care for him after his birth. He was sent away to the mountains to be taken care of by a wet nurse who became like a mother to him. His nurse's husband worked in a quarry that was nestled between mountains. The environment was beautiful and a key to developing Michelangelo's eye for beauty. He would frequently accompany his surrogate father to the mines and watch the workers draw marble from the mountain. Although the workers he witnessed used chisels and hammers, he could see what was possible in the marble. It was in this environment that

Michelangelo learned to see something beautiful in the marble—images of beauty in a hard place, so to speak.

It's a very spiritual activity to take raw material and make something of it. Hard times, hard moments, hard circumstances, hard marble are all opportunities to take raw material and make something of it. Look past the raw facts and see what it could be.

Be like Michelangelo, who said that he chipped away the marble to free the image that he saw in it. You too have the ability to see something good in the hard place. There is never a circumstance or challenge at work, in your home, or in your body that can't be turned into something beautiful. Take the raw and make something amazing. Calling it raw means that it is unfinished, therefore it is subject to change. Everything will surrender to change if you are willing to force the change.

This is a good time to remind you of what Thomas Edison said about invention: "All you need to be an inventor is an imagination and a pile of junk." Don't look at your current challenges and simply call it junk. What could you make with this pile of junk? I know that it's going to be challenging, but let your imagination go. What is possible? Invent something new this week. Let your co-workers stand and watch in awe as you work on the pile of junk until you make it something amazing. It won't be long until others are copying your new formulas and strategies.

This is the second part of the obsession equation; it's what I call the P2 of the equation. It's when your obsession manifests something that is creative genius and worthy of copying. You have developed science that you can perform every time. The solution is now a system that can be taught to others.

The goal is to develop a learned skill from every experience. If you and I can learn something from every experience, good or bad, that can be isolated and developed into a learned skill, then we will be able to intrinsically teach others how to handle or avoid the same.

If you have really learned from something, you would have discovered how to produce the same exact result every time. Not only that, but you would also know how to educate others on how to achieve the same result time and time again. It must transcend knowledge of the skill. This will elevate you into a credible place as an expert.

Let's revisit the equation. We have C2, which is curiosity and creativity. Second, we have skill and craft, which is the SC portion of the equation. Finally, we have the result of the previous two ingredients: professionalism and performance.

Professionalism and performance are the sum total of the obsession equation. Obsession is not simply a heightened state of emotion. Obsession's demands are forceful enough to make a person more calculated, more measurable, more engaged, and fully focused. Obsession forces a person to adjust and readjust until the desired measured results are precisely achieved. Painstaking time and effort are the price for the professional performer.

"Accuracy" and "intentionality" are keywords for the professional performer. God and the universe will not allow sustainable success without this kind of obsessive focus.

An alchemist finds a solution and can perform the same result every time. This is the reason for obsession: to master a subject, to master a problem, to master a science or an art, to master a business, to master a calling.

The performer understands the solution so well that it changes the meaning and how it is done forever. It becomes their art, science, and contribution to society. An obsessed person must finish and complete what they are working on. If it is not finished, it's simply because she was not fascinated by the task. The curiosity and creative juices were not engaged.

Once a person becomes a performer, there must be a professional edge to what they do. It cannot be mediocre.

This is the stage of mastery where your example sets the bar and your perspective sets the rules. Once you have changed the meaning of the raw material, which gives you the absolute authority in that area or sphere, you are the expert.

If you can master it, you can rename it. In some cases, the process takes on your name, as in Mr. Goodyear's case.

At this stage, as a performer of exceptional things, you are able to reproduce the same result every time. This ability will set you apart from the norm and give you recognition as a professional. Your curiosity, creativity, skill, and craft become the standard for professional performance. You are the example, the standard, the yardstick by which everyone measures their results.

This stage is no small feat. It's the reward of your obsession. Many think that the more performance and professionally driven you are, the less sincere you become.

The opposite is true. The more sincere you are, the more intricate and intentional your actions become. This will result in a natural and gradual separation from the crowd. You will begin to display significant distinctions from the rest. This is the unspoken rule of professionalism.

As I mentioned earlier I lived in a home with Olympians. It takes an incredible amount of distinction to go from little league to high school sports and then on to college sports. The margin of separation is significantly larger from those levels of skill and training to the level of Olympian. One of my uncles excelled beyond Olympian and became a professional boxer.

The margin between amateur and professional becomes increasingly obvious. Here the margin between professionals was minutely small. I watched him work diligently to try to get the smallest edge. He worked harder than he had ever worked before. His skill was honed by intentional physical and mental work. He worked exhaustively for small measurement. This is the obsession of a pro. This is the obsession of a world-class performer.

Remember that a performer is someone who can achieve the same result each and every time. Nothing is left to a fluke or accidental success. The obsessed work diligently every day to be more intricate and intentional at what they do. If you see an obsessed person working on their craft, you will quickly recognize the sincerity of every thought and move.

Performance is more sincere because of the amount of practice, excellence, and obsession that it demands to be professional.

Professionals work aggressively toward their goal. They never give place to hesitation. Hesitating is the result of not wanting to stand out. A hesitant person avoids extremes: rich, famous, poor, needy, hot, or cold. They play it safe in the middle. That way they blend in as "I am just like you."

As we discussed in the chapter "Wings of an Ego," hesitation is your enemy. Hesitation will fight against the necessary experimentation that it takes to be creative and curious.

Thomas Edison, along with his team, is credited with inventing thousands of things. This could only be done through experimentation. Thomas Edison invented the phonograph. He figured out a way to capture sound by making impressions on an aluminum cylinder while turning in a counterclockwise direction. When the cylinder was spun clockwise and a needle that was connected to a horn was attached, it played sound. As the needle passed over the impressions, it reproduced the sounds that were captured on the cylinder.

This set a standard for the rest of the world. This one thought unlocked countless ideas. One invention that worked on the same idea was the Spiral Kinetograph, which is one of Edison's lesser-known inventions. It worked on the same principle of a cylinder. Edison thought, *Why can't I do the same thing using pictures?* In essence, by doing this he created a moving-picture camera. In 1893, he built what some think was the first movie studio in his backyard. Edison was an incredible inventor, but unfortunately he was not as good with telling stories through pictures. It is said that his movies lacked entertainment value. Yet, his invention of the Spiral Kinetograph made it possible for great storytellers, such as DW Griffith, to tell their stories and gave us actors like Charlie Chaplin and others in the silent-film era. This little idea eventually gave way to Hollywood. This is an example of how one person's obsession can be developed into professionalism that can consistently perform over and over.

With this level of professionalism and performance, perfectionism is not a leisurely option. I understand that many people are afraid to become perfectionists. Some see it as a curse. Let's be real about it. Someone is working to perfect those things that you and I use daily or desire to buy. The reason we want it is because we know that someone has been so obsessed with the idea that they perfected it. I am writing this portion as I am on an airplane. I only trust this airline and crew because they are perfectionists, professional, and obsessed with getting me to my destination safely. They are committed to performing this each and every time.

Performance and perfectionism cannot be separated. They are one and the same. The world goes around powered by perfectionism. Perfectionism can be a prison if you are not free to stop anytime you want. As a liberated perfectionist, the one thing that empowered me to work on something until perfect, without becoming a freak, was the idea that everything will continue to be developed to another level.

I recently saw a new Mercedes concept car. It is a car that will help them form their ideas and development over the next 30 years. They will not wait to produce a car until they reach that concept. Instead, they will build a robust driving machine now, to the best of their ability, while they form their customers' and employees' minds toward that concept design. This is perfection on the way without an end.

Perfection is not about a finish line; it is about performing at your highest level and being the most professional that you can be each and every time. Only at that level will you notice what can be improved upon.

I realized that I can keep on working on talent, skill, or performance as a part of the process. If there is a flaw, I can keep working on it. Perfectionists should not focus on the finishing but on the process of developing. That is why we are talking about experimenting, not accomplishing. Experiment until you solve the problem perfectly and then experiment more until you understand the science and art of a matter. Then experiment more until you can coach, teach, train, and mentor others to do the same thing. Then experiment more until you are able to systemize and automate it. Then experiment more until you find a better way to do what you just optimized. This is the joy of the journey.

People who are not on a journey find destruction in perfectionism. This is because they think that there is a finish line to their experimentation. Once you finish one thing there is a new starting line.

If you study the work of a sculptor or artist, you will find many unfinished projects. Michelangelo, for instance, was obsessed with his work. Yet you find many works that he started and didn't finish. Does that mean that he was not a perfectionist? Of course not! The signs of perfectionism were forever locked into his physical appearance. He developed a goiter while painting the Sistine Chapel. His posture while painting it was said to have deformed his body. But obsessed and passionate people also know what to put their time into and not into.

Michelangelo's level of professionalism and perfectionism is understood through a story of his reaction to his sculpture of the seated Moses. Once he finished it, he was so engaged by it that he took his mallet and hit it on the knee, commanding it to speak. He was completely invested in the idea that he was releasing Moses from the marble. Michelangelo carved and freed Moses from the rock in such a way that it no longer was rock to him but had a soul that demanded attention.

My objective in this chapter is to speak to the image of greatness within your soul. To dig into your imagination until you are ecstatic with possibilities. My desire is to give permission to your earth-shaking, life-changing, jaw-dropping obsession. I hope that you will live with a fiery-hot passion that comes from an uncommon place within your soul. Give yourself permission to live out loud and be bold doing it. Be obsessed! You have permission to live with obsession. It's the only equation that will set you apart from the crowd.

## Chapter 4

# TABLES ARE TURNING

The coffee industry in Seattle in the '90s was booming. Espresso carts could be found on nearly every corner. Anywhere there was foot traffic you could find an espresso stand. There was a little coffee chain called Starbucks taking off and creating a culture of its own. I didn't drink coffee at the time so I didn't know what the buzz was all about.

During that same time, I moved to Southern California. I immediately noticed that there was something missing in Orange County. Where were all the coffee shops, coffee houses, and espresso carts? I noticed that the only place you could get espresso was at an Italian restaurant or at a 7-Eleven through a single-button automatic espresso/cappuccino maker where every drink tasted the same. I immediately thought that this was a prime opportunity to start an espresso business. I went to the Department of Health in the city. I talked to the street-food vending department. They informed me that they only had one espresso cart in all of Orange County, in Huntington Beach. They didn't have a regulation for an espresso cart, only for hotdog carts.

They made that vendor set up a hotdog cart and convert it to an espresso cart. That was not going to work for the Seattle standard. So I proposed to set a standard and submitted it. They approved and adopted my proposed standard. I was off and running. I built the cart and found a great location at a local car wash. That wouldn't work in most of the country but in SoCal, a car wash is one of the most trafficked locations available. I had many first-time customers but few of them understood authentic coffee. They would complain about the bitter taste. They would ask for a cappuccino but expect a latte. Then they would ask for whipped cream on it. You may think that's right; a mocha should have a little whip. But not just on the mocha—they wanted whipped cream on everything, syrups and whipped cream.

I was doing well but I realized that I spent a lot of time educating the customers about what they were ordering. Then it happened. Starbucks started advertising in Orange County. They came in with diagrams of what a cappuccino was, what a mocha was, what the difference was between a latte and a cappuccino. They hammered the market with education. It took off. I spent hours, days, and months trying to do what they did in a short period of time. They opened a shop and the people were lining up out the door. People couldn't wait to have their drinks.

I clearly understood the lay of the land, that there was room for a new coffee solution for coffee drinkers. I could see what was coming but I didn't possess what was necessary to educate my customer to help them enjoy the product. The supply was there but the demand wasn't. Starbucks educated the community and created a demand that matched their supply.

Time is at hand. Knowing the right time is vitally important to every cause. If an idea is revealed before demand is created, it can be devastating to the business or movement. It is said that pioneers of an idea are never the ones who make the money. It's the people who follow up the idea with innovation, systems, and execution that work toward consumer experience. This is evident in so many booming franchises and companies, such as McDonalds.

Often the pioneer has an idea and a desire to bring it to life, yet they may not have the customer in mind. McDonalds became a giant despite its original upstart. Ray Kroc, the owner of McDonalds, saw an opportunity and took a small local operation to the world because he saw how he could use the customer experience. The key is the customer, not the business.

In order for your product or service to have a customer speak about it to others, you must understand what is appealing to your customer.

It is those who come after the pioneer who eat the fruit of the pioneer's labor. Pioneers can eat the fruit of their labors if they can stay in the game long enough for the word to spread. Why is that? It's a perfect example of my SoCal ideas.

Pioneers must be able to educate and create demand. Most often pioneers are simply trying to see their passion or dream become a reality. They know they can change the world but they are focused on proving their idea more than sharing how the idea will change a customer's life or create the desired lifestyle of the customer. If the consumer cannot see how your idea is going to give them their desired lifestyle, then they will not pay attention long enough to see your good idea. Attention is a payment. People are constantly judging whether or not our thingy is worth the payment of attention that can be given to something else.

There is a story of Jesus of Nazareth describing a famous event in His life. Jesus was on a journey to Jerusalem to visit the temple. He looked around and noticed that the timing was off. He had missed the crowds. The marketplace had already shut down for the day. It was too late for Him to do what He left Bethany to do. He had traveled to Jerusalem to take care of the family business. Instead of trying to make it happen, He turned around and went back to where He came from.

Bethany was a very interesting city. The meaning of the name tells its story. It means "house of dates" or "house of misery or depression." Most people deal with depression and misery because they have not mastered the art of time. So we often feel like we are late and maybe missed an appointment, which is one of the major causes of disappointment.

The next day He made that exact journey again. This time He saw the markets and the merchants selling in the temple. This was the moment Jesus was looking for. He took a whip and drove the merchants out of the temple, saying, "My Father's house is a house of prayer but you have made it a den of thieves." What's the point? The night before He went to the same temple but the timing was off. There was nothing to do. All the merchants were packed up and gone. There was nothing to stand for, no felt need to solve. The next day everything was set for His message.

You often can have the right message and the wrong timing or the right timing and the wrong message. Life can feel like you are making every decision from misery or depression when your readiness doesn't have the necessary opportunities. It can be miserable when what you are looking for seems to be so far away. But when the stars align, everything will fit.

This is what happened to Albert Einstein. For years he lectured on the theory of relativity without any proof. It was only a theory. Then suddenly the sun and moon aligned. Something that hadn't happened for decades happened in his lifetime. In 1919 a solar eclipse took place. This was 14 years after he first presented his paper of the theory of relativity. Einstein's theory was immediately proven by one universal event. He became one of the most famous people alive. He definitely became the face of science. He was launched from being a scientist into pop-star status. Within a year 100 books were published on relativity, even though very few understood it.

You could be in a time of Bethany where the dates don't match your message. At this point, your message is only a lecture. But if you don't give up too soon, you may have an eclipse help launch you and your ideas onto the scene. No matter what your needs may be, there is an eclipse on the schedule. A once-in-a-lifetime event, a once-in-a-lifetime opportunity is coming your way. Don't stay in Bethany! Keep going back to where your event will most likely happen and one day your timing will match your preparedness.

Einstein was born at the perfect time for his curiosity. His father was a leader in what was in their day the equivalent of the dot-com boom in ours. Differential machines were changing the way everything was done. At the turn of the century, people had a sense that anything was possible. Einstein was an extremely focused and determined person. He was unmovable from the task. Years and years preparing for a platform that wasn't ready for him—then suddenly a seemingly divine event catapulted him into stardom overnight. His platform caught up to him.

Winston Churchill also experienced a passion for a platform that hadn't matured yet. Then World War II called on his expertise.

He was being groomed for this very moment. Winston's career history had been up and down until this point. Before World War II, Winston was removed from politics because he was too focused on war. Then he was commissioned to write a book on John Churchill, who led his army to victory over a dictator, King Louis XIV of France. It was a massive task, four volumes of a million-plus words. Winston gave himself to the Marlborough works.

As he was researching the book, he visited Germany and saw Hitler and his Nazis. That is when he realized that Hitler and the Nazi agenda were dangerous. Churchill recognized in Hitler what John Churchill saw in King Louis. Winston said, "Hitler enjoyed war too much."

Hitler was raised as a leader when Germany was experiencing an economic crisis. Poverty and lack was the platform to reveal Hitler. Hitler brought hope to Germany and terror to the rest of the world.

Every leader has a platform designed for them. Could it be that you are being prepared for your platform? Yes, you have experienced some great things, but is it possible that destiny has designed more for you? Everything is beautiful in its time. The era of Churchill, Hitler, and

Einstein was a collision destiny. There were so many major players during this time. They all had something to do with forging humanity for generations to come. Without Hitler, Churchill would have been great but his fame is associated with Hitler. Without Hitler, we wouldn't have the VW bug. Okay, that's pushing it but I wanted to make it clear that good can be found in anything if you look hard enough for it. Without Winston Churchill, many leaders would not be inspired to take their place in history.

Also in this timeframe, we find Sigmund Freud. He was revealed as the father of psychoanalysis. All that was unexplored prior to him. Sigmund Freud rose out of obscurity when he started working with the mentally ill. At the time it was a field for quacks. The common treatments included strange and bizarre things like spinning mentally ill people in chairs hoping to cure them or placing chains on them. There were no real treatments. Freud took on this kind of practice because it was an unexplored field. For him, it was a wide-open subject. During this time he discovered that the human mind had depths to it that had never been researched or talked about. He found that talking to the patient revealed much about the secrets of their thought process and cause for their actions. He would talk with patients about their dreams, during which he discovered the power of the subconscious mind.

At first he was not taken seriously, but as his research revealed the unknown, it became more and more accepted—again, another product of being in the right place, at the right time doing the right thing with the right people, solving the right problem. His platform was an uncommon place in practiced medicine. W. Chan Kim and Renee Mauborgne would say that it was a "Blue Ocean"—a platform with a mature need that needed solutions.

The interesting thing is that Freud, being Jewish, also had to flee from Austria because of Hitler. This era revealed so many leaders. You had the nuclear arms race as well as the Great Depression. It was a perfect platform to reveal leaders. Leaders are not revealed when there are no problems. The world's need for a solution proved these men's leadership abilities. The war, the problem, the challenge before you reveals the leader in you. The platform isn't prepared for problems but for problem solvers. Yes, you will have a problem for the leader in you to solve. Just like in a movie, every protagonist needs an antagonist. Superman needs Lex Luther. God needs a devil. Winston Churchill needed Hitler. Freud needed mental illness. Einstein needed the mysteries of the universe. That's the job of the hero/ leader to discover.

According to Napoleon Hill, each person's problem or challenge brings with it a greater or equal benefit.

Let's look more at the concept of platform maturity. You may be staring your perfect opportunity in the face yet not recognizing that this is the moment you have been preparing for.

You and I have watched people take advantage of the perfect timing in their life. Oprah Winfrey is a perfect example. Her curiosity, talent, willingness to lead the pack, and opportunity aligned. President Obama and now President Trump are examples of platforms that matured. Thomas Edison's communication platform was enabled by the Industrial Age. Henry Ford's platform was the need for the industry to overcome average.

What does your platform look like? Destiny is preparing your platform by preparing you. Destiny is working with her partners to get you ready. Her team is patience, failure, and rejection. Even though a person rising from obscurity into the limelight looks amazing and without challenge, it's usually not the case. Most people who lead have a story. Their story as well as yours includes dreaming for something that demands that you are patient, that forces you to feel yet forget the song of failure. Also, it should go without saying that rejection is a vital part of standing above the rest. Destiny employs these three to make you the powerful leader that you are to become. Your character must match your station.

Recently there was a Netflix series called T*he Crown.* It is based upon the life of Queen Elizabeth. In one of the episodes, there is a perfect example of the shift that takes place when a person is finally in their platform.

Although she was not prepared by normal standards, she was perfect for the platform. At the point of her coronation, there was an obvious change. This is seen in Queen Elizabeth as well as in the coronation of King Saul in Bible days. There is a special separation to those who have a duty and job to be accomplished. Anointing kings and queens to rule has been going on for a long time. Their sovereign station needs them to have a character that doesn't get in the way of their assignment.

As they are being anointed, they are reminded of the power that comes with their duty. This is the same for a priest and the Pope. The Pope's station is an inherited anointing that was supposedly passed from Jesus to His disciple Peter, who was the first pope, down the line until the current pope. The anointing of Jesus was an assignment to destroy the ills of the world. Here it is quoted from the scriptures:

*The Spirit of the Sovereign Lord is upon me because the Lord has chosen me. He has commissioned me to encourage the poor, to help the brokenhearted, to decree the release of captives, and the freeing of prisoners, to announce the year when the Lord will show his favor, the day when our God will seek vengeance, to console all who mourn.*
Isaiah 61:1-2 NET

In Queen Elizabeth's coronation, as is common in all coronations, there is an oath prior to the anointing. It starts off with something like the following: "Promise and Swear to Govern the People of this Kingdom of England and the Dominions thereto belonging according to the Statutes in Parliament Agreed on and the Laws and Customs of the same" (https://en.m.wikipedia.org/wiki/Coronation_of_the_British_monarch).

So I guess the question is, if you were in your coronation service and preparing to be anointed for your destiny and platform, what would be your oath be? "I promise and swear to ______," or, "The Spirit of the Sovereign Lord is upon me to ______."

If you can fill in those blanks, then you can function in the anointing to cure those ills. This is what you are being prepared for. You could be the very person who takes the company that you work with to its next level. All of the struggles and training before now have prepared you for this moment. You are the destined solution to some problem. Find the problem and cure it. This is the way of an alchemist. The is the way of an experimentalist. They work to find a solution. You are anointed to find solutions. Destiny is counting on you to find the solution.

Henry Kissinger said, "Leaders must invoke an alchemy of great vision." In our modern day, we are experiencing a crisis on all fronts. Social, spiritual, and economic ills threaten the human condition. We need a new move of leadership. We need risk-takers. We need a new breed of entrepreneurs, ones that are willing to experiment with new ideas until solutions are found. We need millennials and Gen Z leaders who will race for solutions. Social, spiritual, and economic entrepreneurs practice alchemy to solve the ills at hand.

## YOUR ANOINTING + PROBLEM = PLATFORM

I know that all of this platform and destiny talk could sound random, but in economics it's called a Kondratiev wave or a supercycle. This is an example of a Kondratiev wave.

Supercycles are 40- to 50-year cycles; some economists say 80 years.

Every organization experiences cycles or waves. The economist Nikolai Kondratiev, who promoted free-market enterprise in the Soviet Union, theorized that Western capitalist economies have a boom to depression cycle of 50-60 years.

As you can see, the waves follow the cycle. We would currently fall into the informational/technology wave. It appears that every economy or ecosystem has cycles where new thought is introduced and then exhausted. There is then a need for a new cycle based upon new thought to build progressively upon the previous thought. This is the

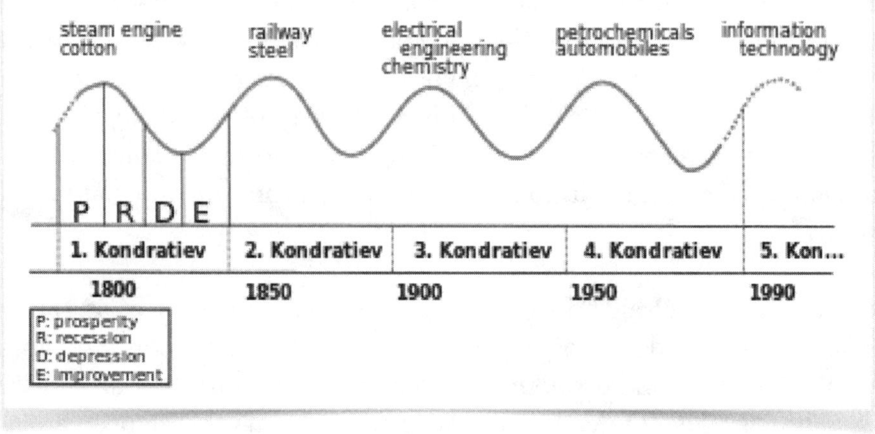


process that Nikolai Kondratiev systematically described as PRDE. PRDE stands for prosperity, recession, depression, and improvement.

You can expect this cycle in everything. Even when you buy a new car. You feel overjoyed with it at first. As time moves along you recess on it a little bit when you notice that there are things that you would change. Then you depress it by playing it down or recognizing the flaws until you must make modifications or buy a new car. This happens in relationships, with jobs, with everything. It's because this cycle is psychological and will always be with humanity. If we understand the cycles, we can also flow with the cycles and make the best of it. The wave descends at the peak of its prosperity. It doesn't plateau. It starts to recess, then depress, and will ultimately need to rebirth and reemerge as a new event.

The interesting thing to me is that each generation has the privilege of producing its own revival or renaissance by developing new thoughts while standing on the shoulders of previous thought leaders. Revivals are corrugated. They flow in waves. As you look at the diagram, you will see a dying industry and a new frontier within the same wave. You might think that the new frontier begins when it hits the peak, but it actually starts when the previous industry begins to fail and decline.

The platform for the new thing is at the bottom of the wave. Early adopters have started climbing on during the downward slope of the previous industry and the upward slope of the new. What am I saying? You are maturing for a cycle, whether in your industry, in your home, or in your company. You will feel the great pull toward the new thing while everyone is still clambering for the current. You will be frustrated with a vivid vision for what is next while everyone else is talking about what is now. You will have to weather the storm of criticism as you wait for your platform to mature. You will have to spend time as an esoteric fanatic prophesying something that is hard for others to see.

If you stay the course and don't give up, you will be in position for the platform to mature. The danger is that when you are in obscurity you try to fold and conform, or even worse, become a bitter martyr. Stay solution-oriented. You are not heralding for your own sake. You are on an anointed crusade for a greater good. To cure the ills in your industry, society, and family, you must stay the course. These challenges are designed to cause the alchemist in you to experiment.

We need to experiment with what we have in order to see if we are able to change what needs healing. Deep thought is expressed in testing the limits. Reach out; stretch out; dig deep; look higher. System-changing solutions are not found with low-hanging fruit. You must go for new growth using well-tested truths and new thoughts. Abraham Maslow said, "With a tree, all the growth takes place at the growing tips. Humanity is exactly the same. All the growth takes place in the growing tip: among that one percent of the population. It's made up of pioneers, the beginners. That's where the action is."

I believe that a new mindset and psychology are needed in order to make change happen. When I speak of an alchemist, I am referring to a process of thinking, not the medieval activities. The meaning of alchemy (āl'kə-mē) is "a medieval philosophy and early form of chemistry whose aims were the transmutation of base metals into gold, the discovery of a cure for all diseases, and the preparation of a potion that gives eternal youth. The imagined substance capable of turning other metals into gold was called the philosophers' stone."

The chief aim of an alchemist is to discover a cure for diseases. Bob Proctor says that you must hyphenate disease when talking about it. You, as an alchemist, are to desire to cure all diseases. If there is dis-ease at home, then you, as an alchemist, can bring about a cure. If there is dis-ease at work, then you, as an alchemist, can cure dis-ease. The key to success in any area is to find a cure for dis-ease.

The second psychological thought of an alchemist is to keep things lively, enthusiastic, and energetic. The medieval strategy was to create a potion for eternal life. In our postmodern world, your charisma is the potion. Hope and faith are contagious. Possibility and optimism are potentially contagious. Fill a room with hope, faith, possibility, and optimism and within a short time people will be oozing with youthful zeal and excitement to figure out the cure to any problem.

The third thought of the alchemist is that they believe in the impossible. They believe that there is a key solution, a master key, to solving the most impossible problems. They sought the philosophers stone; with this stone they could turn common metal into gold. I would love to have a team of people who believe that they could turn anything that is common to gold. I would love to have someone on the team who believes that they can think through a problem and come up with a solution. I like to have philosophical thinkers on the team. If you don't have anyone on the team asking "What if?" or "Do you think that this might work?" you don't have what Maslow called pioneers and beginners. Therefore, you don't have philosophers, and consequently, you don't have new thoughts and the tip-of-the-tree growth. I love talking with our millennial and Gen Z team members. They don't have enough experience to be experts, so they are amazing philosophers. They believe that you can turn normalcy into gold. They are alchemists.

If you have all of these elements, you will discover a love potion #9 that can change the world. Even if you don't, you will discover some amazing things trying. Medieval alchemists discovered many of our current tools and solutions trying to turn common metals into gold, even though they had very little success in achieving their lofty goal of turning lead into gold. Alchemists invented early forms of some of the laboratory equipment used today, including beakers, crucibles, filters, and stirring rods. They also discovered and purified a number of chemical elements, including mercury, sulfur, and arsenic. And the methods they developed to separate mixtures and purify compounds by distillation and extraction are still important.

Experimentation with new thoughts for curing dis-ease will ultimately generate usable solutions.

Earlier we looked at a story of Jesus turning over tables because the timing was right for that to happen. Destiny is preparing you for tables to be turned. Things are about to turn around.

In order for tables to turn in your favor, you will need to be willing to pay attention to the timing of the circumstance that is at hand. You must be ready to turn the table over. Disruption is the leader of change. You will have to look at old systems and ask new questions.

Tables are turning, we are moving into a new era if you believe in economic waves. Technology is speeding up these super-cycles. Something new and fresh is needed in leadership and in industry. The Internet has changed the playing field and has made the world flat, so to speak. Get ready for your platform to mature.

Everything is subject to change. Companies that are sweeping industries are using strategic alignments and collaboration to create disruption. They're using their strengths to engage the cure and disrupt the market. They are using strategic alignments to reposition themselves for disruption. A part of paying attention is to be aware of strategic alignments that better position you for a maturing platform. You may not have the full solution but you can multiply your potential through collaboration and alignments.

Use your philosopher stone (your brain) and recognize what's coming next before it arrives. Be your own prophet and futurist. Tables are turning for you. Begin to turn over some tables yourself. Get rid of old time wasters. Turn over energy zappers. Don't waste any of your talents or abilities investing in what once worked. Find the ills and dis-ease you are anointed to cure and work on it. Harness all of your abilities to make a difference where you are—at work, at home, in your community, in your country, even globally. We are moving into another era of stand-out leaders. Take your place, turn over tables, because tables are turning.

Alchemist revolution is at hand! Make something happen!

## Chapter 5

# HARNESSING

*The heavens are the heavens of the LORD, But the earth He has given to the sons of men.*
Psalm 115:16 (NASB)

I once heard Bob Proctor say that science is the study of the natural world and religion is the study of the inner world. I believe that we should have a strong grasp on both the study of the natural world and the unseen inner world.

## MAUI VS BRUSSELS

I have been to Maui. It is beautiful. The water is gorgeous. The trees are amazing. The sunsets are out of this world. But I couldn't help but feel like it was missing something. My mind kept going back to our last vacation in Amsterdam, Paris, and Brussels. My wife and kids gave me an amazing birthday treat and took me on this three-country tour. They said no work allowed. To this day it was the most enjoyable vacation that I have ever experienced.

So, as I sat at a five-star hotel pool that was just footsteps from the beach in Maui, I couldn't understand what was missing. Why was I comparing this trip to Brussels? The first day in Maui we walked to the beach and saw a family of dolphins swimming by. The next day a huge, I mean huge, sea turtle came swimming along with us. I still couldn't figure out was wrong. Then suddenly I realized what it was. I was looking at everything that was naturally beautiful in Maui, all the works of God, but what I didn't see were the amazing works of the hands of man. Where is the amazing architecture?

In Paris, I saw the Eiffel Tower.

In Amsterdam, I saw museums filled with works of art and beautiful buildings that took decades to build. I saw intricate canal designs that allow boats to travel from city to city.

In Brussels, I went to La Grand Place and saw the town hall as the centerpiece.

In 1420, Jacob van Thienen completed the West wing of this edifice, and in 1444 Charles the Bold laid the first stone to the East wing. The East wing was constructed by Guillaume (Willem) de Vogel. What an amazing thought: three different people working on one project—each person imagining that stone, metal, and wood could be made into something magnificent.

The earth belongs to the children of man. Human potential is unmatched by any other creature on the earth. The power of humans to use their minds to create something from raw material is amazing—using rudimentary material and their logic and problem-solving faculties to create something that could withstand time, use, and weather patterns.

Pioneers took wood and created cabins, then the next pioneers saw how to improve on the cabin as a home and make a larger family dwelling—each person recognizing what was previously done yet still finding a way to improve on it until ultimately we have the person who dreamed of building a skyscraper. This is much different than a beaver that also uses wood to build its home. You will never come upon a beaver in the woods building a skyscraper. You and I have been given a gift. We have the power on Earth to make things, to create, and to improve upon what has been created. You have an unlimited capacity.

Creativity learns to separate problems from any possible solution by turning and turning new and fresh ideas in the mind until you see another possible idea that would work. After creating something new, you will ultimately realize a better way to innovate it. Upon testing it you see the flaw; you turn it around more and more in your thinking until you see another possible solution. Let's call this creating with chaos.

Creating with chaos is a design, not a design flaw. Being a creationist, I believe that chaos was purposefully designed to help develop our creative faculties. The world was created with and through chaos. The Hebrew words used are *tohu* and *bohu*, which mean "void" and "empty." Void and empty are perfect workspaces for possibility thinkers. A mom is working in a kitchen. She keeps passing by an empty cookie jar, and something in her mind says that empty jar needs cookies. She then looks into the pantry to see if she has flour. She does! She then looks into the fridge to see if she has eggs. She does! She then looks in another cabinet to see if there is sugar, or monk fruit for the healthier mom types. It's there also. What about milk? No, she is out of milk. Maybe her next-door neighbor has some milk she can borrow. Once she has all of the raw materials, she then mixes all of the raw material together. She adds a little heat and within a short time the cookies are finished and the cookie jar is no longer empty.

I have a household of artists—something that has been passed down from my father-in-law, a world-class painter in his youth. My kids look at a blank canvas and dream of how to fill that void. They see yellows and blues and lavenders in the empty canvas in a way that makes a recognizable image. I see a tan cloth on a frame. When they look at that canvas they want to do something with it. When I look at it I want to walk past it.

Your mind and heart are your canvas. The areas of your life that appear to be *tohu* and *bohu* are your workspace. If God created everything perfect, what did He leave for us to discover and to develop our potential? No, the earth belongs to the children of man.

Empty and void are chaos only to those who do not possess the possibility of what it could become. Fruitless, passionless, creative-lacking people see challenges and mess as chaos. Creatives and possibility-thinkers see empty and void as opportunities to express creativity. It is a proven reality that everything leans towards chaos.

Last year I was in Holland. A news report came out about how an elderly man was reunited with the car he had lost many years before. Years ago he parked his car in a specific garage and when he returned to where he thought he parked it, the car was gone. He assumed that the car was stolen. But, no, he went to the wrong parking space. Years later it was returned to him. The car would no longer start or run, the tires were flat, the paint was destroyed, yet it never moved from its place. You would think that it would have stayed in perfect condition.

This is impossible because of thermodynamics. The function of thermodynamic variables, as temperature, pressure, or composition, is a measure of the energy that is not available for work during a thermodynamic process. The heat of the sun, change of temperature from the wind, and other elements cause things to break down.

This is very similar to what causes the wave in the super-cycle. A problem arises and then the creative and inventive process reveals a solution. The solution moves from obscurity to normalcy. Then other problems are revealed to start the process all over again.

There are chaotic moments in life that are perfectly suited to reveal your creative abilities.

I believe that I have the power of creation within me. This power is far superior to chaos. Your God-given ability is to create when there is a void or emptiness. Scripture describes the Creator as the Father of Light who has no variations or shadow of turning. In essence, this statement means that God is unmoved by the laws of thermodynamics. He doesn't change with times, seasons, or circumstances. There is not a measure of pressure that can change Him. He always has more than enough energy to deal with anything that would attempt to break Him down. There is no *aposkiasma tropē*, which means His shadow never changes. Shadows are created by a greater light overshadowing a subject. If there is no greater light, then you cannot cast a shadow. He only has light.

Why is this important? Because you are the image of God. You have the power not to allow anything to overshadow you. You have the ability to keep turning outward to keep growing.

Entropy is the part of thermodynamics that causes things to lean toward chaos. Dictionary.com defines this as "a thermodynamic quantity representing the unavailability of a system's thermal energy for conversion into mechanical work, often interpreted as the degree of disorder or randomness in the system or the lack of order or predictability; gradual decline into disorder."

"Entropy" comes from the two Greek words *en*, which is the word "in," and *trope*, which means "confusion" or "shame." In science, it describes a system that turns in on itself because it lacks the energy to keep it from doing so. It's a closed system.

For example, the paint on that car that was parked for years starts to break down and deteriorate because it doesn't have enough energy to compete against the energy of the sun. A tree is the opposite in that it is an open system. It's alive! It has life from the nutrients it gets from the ground and sunlight. It has energy flowing in and flowing out in the form of $H_2O$. A closed system has nothing flowing in and nothing flowing out. An open system has energy flowing in and energy flowing out. It's both living and life-giving. The only way to deal with chaos is to be an open system like a tree. It takes the energy from the sun and converts it to something that is life-giving. The sun is damaging to something that cannot convert its energy and make something better.

You have the potential to be a closed system or an open system. You can let the chaos damage you or you can bring order to it and make something good out of it.

The statement that there is no shadow of turning relates to the fact that there is no chaotic circumstance that has more energy than you. It can't overwhelm you. You have enough energy to turn it around, to make something life-giving from it. This is the power of harnessing.

Chaos happens when a plan is not in place to intentionally stop it from moving toward destruction.

*Closed System*

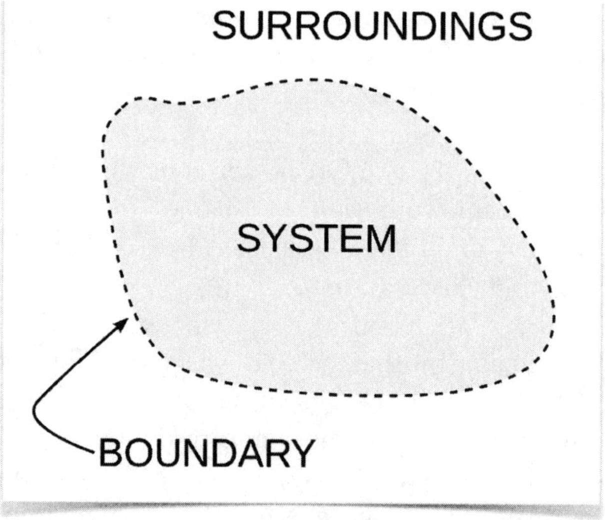


When you don't possess the energy necessary to affect your surroundings, you are a closed system left to the effects of your surroundings.

*Open System*

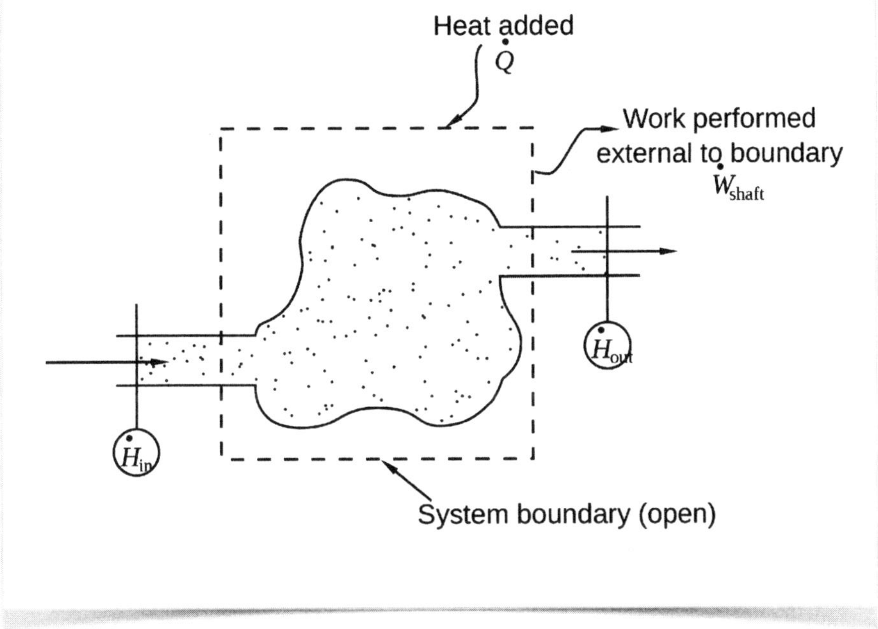


On the other hand, when you possess the energy within, you will not only have the power to resist the external pressures of your surroundings from driving you into chaos, but you will also be empowered to add to the surroundings around you.

A closed system can also be something that takes in life but doesn't give out life. For example, during the dot.com boom, many entrepreneurs became wealthy at rapid speeds. Many of those entrepreneurs soon became sick with flu-like symptoms. At first, researchers thought that the sickness was associated with sitting and looking at a computer too long. They soon realized that it was associated with their rapid increase in wealth and influence. They called it "affluenza." Affluenza is "the negative psychological or behavioral effects of having or pursuing wealth, as irresponsible acts and feelings of self-doubt or guilt or the excessive materialism or desire for wealth, associated with negative effects," according to dictionary.com. The problem with the dot.

com affluenza victim was that they were taking in much but giving little. They were a closed system. They needed to have a generosity that matched their affluence.

It's like a deep-sea diver. The pressure increases the deeper the diver goes into the sea. The internal pressure of his suit must be regulated to match the external pressure or else it will implode on the diver. In order for the diver to survive, he must take in air and release air. It's the power to harness energy and use it.

There must be an intake that gives life, but there must also be an outflow that gives life.

There is an amazing word from Hebrew scripture that describes this process wonderfully. It's the word *kivshua*. It's translated as "subdue." It was used when God said to man to be fruitful, subdue, and have dominion on the earth. He breathed into man and gave him the power to subdue. The more precise translation of the word *kivshua* is "to harness it," to bring under control so that you can use it. I believe that you and I are empowered to harness elements and circumstances to bring them under our control and use them to create a better life on Earth.

We possess the ability to nurture what has seed until it reaches its potential. We harness rock and give it a greater purpose. Rock is rock until you and I choose to make something greater of it. Metal is material until a manufacturer makes it into an intravenous needle that can deliver medicine. Chaos is problematic until we find a solution to subdue it.

Peter Drucker said it this way: "The entrepreneur always searches for change, responds to it, and exploits it as an opportunity." The earth belongs to mankind.

## MAKE IT HAPPEN

Humanity has been proving this statement since the dawn of time. Let's look at four basic elements that humanity has learned to harness and use to better our quality of life. This same power is available to you to subdue an element and/or chaotic circumstance and make it usable.

Throughout the centuries mankind has successfully harnessed elements of the earth to better humanity and produce a better quality of life. The four obvious elements are water, earth, air, and fire.

Allow me to show you a few examples of the human potential to harness a raw material of the earth to better humanity.

My objective in doing this is to convey to you that you possess the same innovation and resourcefulness even though the material may be different. If it can be done with earth, air, water, and fire, then it can be done with anything—that is, if you activate your imagination, creativity, and curiosity.

## EARTH

The first example is the oil tycoon John D. Rockefeller. He was the founder of the Standard Oil Company, which refined oil into usable material. Once it was extracted from the ground, it was then refined into kerosene and oil. He extracted and refined so much from the earth that he became the richest man in the United States. At one point he controlled 90 percent of the wealth in the country. He became so powerful that in 1911 the U.S. Supreme Court ruled that the Standard Oil Company be dismantled. This ruling resulted in 34 separate entities. Many would be recognized today such as Exxon, Mobil, and Chevron. This ruling created an opportunity for him to increase until he became the first billionaire of the United States of America.

Rockefeller used raw material from the earth to change the world. His wealth was estimated to be 2 percent of the U.S. economy, reaching approximately $336 billion dollars in 1913. Yet, his wealth creation wasn't merely in financial gain. He used his wealth to be a social entrepreneur. His generosity made changes in medicine, education, and scientific research. His foundations achieved substantial progress in medical research and were instrumental in finding cures for hookworm and yellow fever. Yellow fever was nearly eradicated in the United States because of his research.

Rockefeller's ability to harness kerosene from the ground only gave him more confidence that he could refine more products from the ground. Once the automobile came along, with his ability to harness oil, it made it possible to harness gasoline and fuel cars.

## WATER

What about the element of water? That is very difficult to harness. Yet, even as a child, we learn to harness it. When I was young we went to Mount Rainier in Washington state. We found streams flowing with fresh water on the mountain. If we were thirsty, we would simply kneel beside the stream and reach into the water with our cupped hand, bringing as much water as we possibly could to our mouth to drink.

I read a story of a warrior who separated his battle-ready soldiers from those who were not ready by simply watching how they drank from a stream. He had them go to the river and drink water. As he observed them drinking, he noticed that the majority of them got down on all fours to drink like a dog. Only 300 of the thousands kneeled down and brought the water to their mouth. I conclude that the 300 had enough sense to stay aware and not put their head completely down, making it possible to see an enemy. I couldn't help but think that they seemed smarter than the others. They showed a little better aptitude through their ability to harness water and move it.

Some of the greatest warriors in history were the Romans. Yet, that is not all they used their wit and creativity for. They also mastered the art of harnessing water and moving it to areas of their city that needed it.

It is a well-known fact that the Roman's enjoyed their bathhouses—leisure that couldn't be facilitated by the city's local water source. The local city's water was polluted and carried water-born diseases. So they used aqueducts to move water from far distances to mills, farms, and, of course, bathhouses.

The Romans constructed a very elaborate water system under the city. By the third century AD, Rome had eleven aqueduct systems supplying an urban community of over one million people, including farms, bathrooms, gardens, mills, and households. The Romans constructed the first aqueduct in 312 BC, commissioned by the censor Appius Claudius Caecus, which he named the Aqua Appia.

If humans really have a superpower, it is the ability to harness whatever is needed to answer a problem. Let's think about aqueduct construction. It was made of stone and was able to move water from one place to another place in order to solve the polluted water-supply issue with fresh and palatable water for citizens and livestock. Today we bottle water in BP-free water bottles to supply flavored water, PH-enhanced

water, spring water, artisan water, or sparkling water. There is always another solution to the current problem.

You and I have the power to harness water. What else could we use our powers to harness? How about air?

## AIR

As I mentioned before, when I was a child I watched a lot of television. But my TV watching wasn't limited to *Batman and Robin* or *Kung Fu*. I also liked nature shows like *The Wild Kingdom* and *National Geographic*. My favorite was any show that featured Jacques Cousteau. He exposed me to a world that wasn't readily available. Jacques was unique in that he wanted the world to experience this world as he had so often. He created movies and TV shows to expose the rest of the world to the sea. Philippe Cousteau, Jr., Jacques's grandson, said this about him: "Pioneers are obsessed with the new . . . new worlds to be discovered. My grandfather was Jacques Cousteau, a pioneer of ocean exploration and the co- inventor of scuba diving.

Back in the 1940s when he tested out his invention which allowed humans to swim freely in the ocean with a portable air source for the

first time in history, very little of the ocean had been explored let alone captured on film." Jacques harnessed air in a portable source and allowed people to dive deeper and longer than ever before. The prototypes were aqua lungs in 1943. They were featured in the film *Épaves* (*Shipwrecks*).

The current technology used in scuba diving is made possible because of the discoveries of Jacques Cousteau. He was able to harness air in such a way that it has enabled thousands of people to experience the sea. Let's look at one more. Fire!

## FIRE

Because I travel often, I find myself up late in strange hotels. Occasionally, I find myself awake late at night channel surfing. Most of the time I land on some kind of nature show. Recently, I found myself watching two guys who had been dropped off in the middle of the ocean to survive as if they had been shipwrecked. After a short time, they discovered a remote island. They had a very limited supply. The plan was to leave them with supplies that a shipwreck would provide.

Once they landed on the island they quickly listed their needs. They knew that they would need food, fresh water, and fire. They searched the island for food and found a few things that would do. They also came up with an idea for how to catch fish in the ocean. Yet, the only water source was the ocean's salt water. They quickly realized that they would have to distill salt water in order to have fresh water. They needed fire in order to do so. They also needed a fire so that they could stay warm throughout the night and keep away predators, but they didn't have any matches.

You already know what is next.

They searched for wood that they could use to create a fire. They used two pieces of wood to create friction by spinning one stick in a circular motion into the other piece of wood. After a few minutes, the wood started a smoldering ember, which they placed into a ball of dried grass. Then one of the survivalists blew on the ember until it lit the dried grass. At this time they added the burning grass to a pile of wood that then turned into a fire. That was a perfect example of the ability to harness the power of fire.

Fire is said to be the first element that mankind harnessed. The ability to control fire changed everything. Just like the two survivors, fire allowed mankind to be warm at will. They didn't have to wait for a fire to spontaneously combust to get warm. The mastery of the power of fire enabled mankind to cook food, to protect their camps from beasts, and also to be active longer in the day.

## EARLY MANKIND

In primitive stories, lightning struck from the sky and lit a tree, allowing mankind to use fire. Even in the Bible, we see that the first mention of fire is when it fell from heaven to light an altar of worship. If the introduction of fire to mankind came from heaven, man did a great job harnessing and mastering it. Today we have lighters and matches. If you are an outdoorsy type, you can use flint or two

pieces of wood. Mankind found uses and ways to re-create its effect at will. Either way, humanity now controls fire and uses it to better our quality of life.

We, meaning mankind, are currently in an age where we are becoming smarter and more knowledgeable about anything that we are curious about. Information is important to our development, and Google has harnessed the power of information and placed it at our fingertips.

We have been given the earth as our inheritance and we can make anything of it that we imagine. Zuckerberg wanted a way to connect at a greater level and through Facebook has harnessed the power of connectivity. Boeing and Airbus harnessed the power of force and lift to transport people around the world.

Success is about harnessing, mastering, and repeatedly using elements and powers on Earth to solve social, economic, spiritual, and lifestyle needs.

Paul the apostle, the writer of the book of Romans, clearly gives an image of our human potential. Paul writes, "That's why I don't think there's any comparison between the present hard times and the coming good times. The created world itself can hardly wait for what's coming next" (Romans 8:18-19, MSG).

Hard times are not to deter us, but hard times determine us. We develop a hope-filled determination when we have to believe and dream of what could be.

Black American slaves found joy in believing that there was coming to them a better day. They wrote and sang songs with lyrics filled with the hope of a savior, songs of a deliverer who would come to save them from their affliction. That's what spirituality is all about; it's faith, hope, and joy based upon a belief that something better can be had.

Although music was used to uplift the spirits of slaves, an even greater hope for them was found in the underlying message of the negro-spirituals. These spirituals contained information about escape plans and escape routes. They communicated through negro-spirituals how they were going to be delivered from bondage—hope, joy, and action all in one song.

An encyclopedia.com article, "History of African American Music," gives more detail: "Many of the songs offered coded messages. Some, like "Follow the Drinking Gourd," "Steal Away," and "Wade in the Water," contained coded instructions for an escape to the North. Others, like "(Sometimes I Feel Like) A Motherless Child" and "I'm Troubled in Mind," conveyed the feelings of despair that black slaves felt. The spirituals also served as critiques of slavery, using biblical metaphors to protest the enslavement of black people.

Such protest can be found in the lyrics of "Go Down, Moses":

*Go down, Moses*
*Way down to Egypt land*

*Tell ol' Pharaoh*
*Let my people go.*

Moses and Pharaoh were a common theme in many of the negro spirituals. The slaves related to Israel's desire to be free from Pharaoh. That's not all they had in common with Israeli slaves. Every African-American slave learned new skills and trades in their slavery, just as Israeli slaves did in Egypt.

In Egypt, the slaves learned how to make bricks and build large edifices. This later came in handy for their deliverance. Even Moses the deliverer was delivered himself through the skillful craftsmanship of his sister. The basket that he sailed in down the river as a baby was held together by pitch and tar that was also used to build for the Egyptians—something that she learned from her slavery.

Additionally, in the desert after the slaves were set free, Moses led them to make articles of worship through skills that they developed as slaves. They were very skilled artisans. They were able to craft amazing works of art and worship from a single piece of gold through the process of beating it with a hammer, forming it into a perfectly proportioned piece of ornamentation or furniture. One specific piece, called the mercy seat, had two angels whose wings stretched outward. Can you imagine the skill necessary to use a hammer to form one piece of metal into a beautifully sculpted angel statue with wings revealing the detail of each feather on the wing? All of their hardworking past was being put to good use for their future. Skills developed from 400-plus years of slavery made them first-class artists.

In the same way, African-American slaves developed and honed their musical skills while singing on the plantations of America. They hand-crafted instruments that were most likely crude yet functional. These instruments became more refined over time and ultimately became common instruments used in blues, bluegrass, gospel, and country music.

The encyclopedia article noted earlier also claims the following: "Some of the slaves were able to bring musical instruments with them or build new ones in this country. The 'banja' or 'banshaw,' now known as the banjo, was one of the African instruments that continued to be built and played in America. Africans in America also fashioned numerous types of drums and percussion instruments from whatever materials they could gather. Slaveholders, however, eventually discovered that African slaves were using drums to communicate among themselves and by the 1700s, drums had been banned on many plantations."

It is believed that the musical influences from African-American slaves moved from the plantation to Motown. The gifts forged in slavery became the gifts that forged their future.

When you can look at a circumstance, determining that something better could be had, you can no longer be limited and controlled by those circumstances. There is a force within you, a power that has been granted to you to overcome all limitations—no matter if they are emotional, natural, or material limitations. You'll rise above it! You are able to manipulate the moment into something that is usable.

There are always skills being developed when hardship and pressure are evident. Creative genius finds its way through the muck and mire of limitations.

Maybe your current limitations seem like slavery. Yet, if you look closely, you may find that a skill or ability has been formed through it, a skill and ability that will enable you to harness something that changes your life forever. Keep a possibility mindset during your setback and you will find yourself being set up. This is what we see happening with Winston Churchill in our next chapter.

Chapter 6

# CONCOCTING CURES

*All it takes for evil to exist is for good men to do nothing.*
Unknown

As Winston Churchill campaigned against Hitler and the Third Reich, he soon realized that it was not a task to be done with the resources within his grasp. He decided that he needed to enlist the alliance of the U.S.A. He reached out to Franklin D. Roosevelt, who at first refused to participate because the U.S. was at war with Japan.

Winston Churchill wouldn't take no for an answer. He sent FDR a special edition leather-bound signed copy of his latest written work, *Marlboro.* FDR was a historian like Winston, and soon after receiving it, devoured the writing. After reading the volume, FDR aligned with Great Britain to stand against Hitler.

If the U.S., in addition to other allies, hadn't joined the fight against Hitler, Hitler would have had the military strength to continue his assault against Europe, Africa, and the whole world.

If good people do not stand up against evil, evil's craving for stealing, killing, and destroying will dominate. If people who are of good character and values turn a blind eye, evil will win.

Men and women who are good at what they do can never sit around and watch failure and/or oppression. They will be called out of the shadows and into the light to assist in overcoming oppression. They will feel the need to enter the conflict no matter how much they don't want to.

Einstein, a pacifist, joined the nuclear race to help the U.S.A. once he realized what Hitler would do if Hitler accomplished it first. Einstein knew that Hitler would use nuclear power to control the world.

When you face a crisis or opposition for the first time, all solutions are virtually experimental. It's the essence of alchemy. You go to the lab, so to speak, looking to find a cure. You try this and, if it doesn't work, you try that; and if that somewhat worked, you add a little of this and take away a little of that. Then you try it again until you find the cure. That is how experimental success works. It's a kind of alchemy. It's about searching for a solution. It's like concocting a cure from the resources that you currently have access to.

Concocting cures is fundamental to an entrepreneurial spirit, to being a pioneer. Both entrepreneurs and alchemists spend time experimenting to find the solution. You too can tap into a kind of creative genius by activating your curiosity. An alchemist tests things and tries things. An experimentalist is more afraid of not trying than they are of failing. They use their curiosity and entrepreneurial mindset to solve economic, social, and spiritual ills of society.

"Perhaps" is a word that should be familiar to all of us. "Perhaps" is a part of the vocabulary of an experimentalist. "Perhaps" is the mindset of the scientist who experiments. "Perhaps" is the power of persuasion that every leader leans into to try something new. "Perhaps" helped pioneers daily set their coordinates in order to set sail to discover new lands. "Perhaps" in the principle of business is what a startup writes into their business plan to get things started. We call it a forecast.

There was a young man by the name of Jonathan who was facing a difficult circumstance. His father, Saul, was the king of a defeated kingdom. Their enemy defeated them to the point that they were controlled by their enemy. The enemy sent raiders to their cities and conquered them. Once they defeated them, they made a decree that they wouldn't allow Jonathan and King Saul to have any blacksmiths in their kingdom. The mindset behind that is that they would never be able to start a war against them without swords and spears.

Every time they would try to start a forge, the Philistines would send a troop to destroy the forge. If King Saul needed tools for agriculture, they needed to go to the Philistines for them. Because Israel was monopolized by the Philistines, the Philistines charged exaggerated prices for these tools. The price of these tools and the cost to sharpen them were too expensive for them, so if Israel ever decided to go to war they wouldn't have a sword or spear. Only two people in the whole kingdom of Israel had a sword or spear: King Saul and his son Jonathan.

One day Jonathan had a wild idea. It was as if he was completely fed up with being controlled by someone else. It was as if Jonathan couldn't handle watching the Philistines controlling every one of their decisions. He was sick and tired of watching the families in his territory being tormented. So he said to his helper, "Come on, let's go over to the Philistine garrison that is opposite us." What did this mean? The only way to break through and break from something is to oppose it. Jonathan realized that his enemy would continue to control them until they decided to do the opposite of what they had been doing.

That is the first thing we all need to do when we stand up against what's been limiting us. We need to do the opposite. There is an old *Seinfeld* episode where George has discovered that the key to his success is to do the opposite of what he would normally do. This is very true though—maybe not as exaggerated as what was displayed in the TV show. But you and I definitely must do the opposite. You can always make excuses for doing something new because of fear. Instead, do the opposite. Do it afraid! Sometimes that decision is very difficult because it is far from your norm, even your family norm.

This was true in Jonathan's case. While Jonathan was making this decision, his father was enjoying himself under a pomegranate tree. Saul was comfortable with containment. Saul was comfortable with his people being controlled because it didn't affect his lifestyle. King Saul was enjoying the finest things in life while the people that he led were being tormented. Saul had 600 guards that kept him secure while his people didn't have any safety or protection.

Yet his son Jonathan could not feel comfortable with being controlled any longer. I believe that we have a generation of young leaders, millennial entrepreneurs, who are like Jonathan. They will not sit around and watch people suffer when they can do something about it.

The opening quote speaks loudly to this thought: "All it takes for evil to prevail is for good people to do nothing." When these millennial entrepreneurs see oppression and social ills in the earth, they will feel as if it's a call to action. As Jonathan and his helper were running toward the camp of their enemy, Saul had no idea what his son was up to. In order for Jonathan to reach the camp of his enemy, he had to climb a steep cliff. This is apropos for anyone who desires to confront something that has been controlling them. To oppose the issue is like climbing a steep hill. The steepness of the climb will often deter a person who is not determined to make change happen.

The steepness of the climb did not deter Jonathan. His response to his helper was, "Come on, let's go over to the garrison of these uncircumcised men. Perhaps the Lord will intervene for us." The power of the word "perhaps" is what gave them the courage to pursue the impossible.

The way this story ends is with Jonathan and his helper climbing the cliff and defeating 20 men within a small confined space of a half acre. This quick victory sent intimidation into the rest of the enemy's camp and they fled. The footsteps of the opposing army could be heard as far as King Saul's comfortable tent. The sound startled him to his feet and aroused him to engage in the battle. Sometimes all it takes for evil to be overcome is for someone to take initiative.

The hardest part of doing something new is to get it started. Most people are intimidated with getting things started but will gladly follow once it's going. If you are strategizing and planning change in your company or organization, the objective should be to get quick and noticeable results. This will cause people to come alongside you to achieve the objective. Once you have good results, you will clearly know how to help others get onboard and how to scale the business or project to the next level.

I enjoy going to leadership training and leadership conferences because I get to hear the results of successful people who stepped out on something as simple as "perhaps." When they teach us and share their case studies, they don't say that they stepped out on a "perhaps," but the reality is that after the "perhaps" works we look smart and we now have a formula for someone else to follow us up the cliff. The experience gives us an expert position to teach others how to experience the same success from our proven techniques. But they never tell us how to do what has never been done, how to move on a calculated hunch and risk.

The truth is that most leaders go into a private planning meeting hoping for a solution. They sit around a table discussing their hopes as calculated risk. They do this until they come up with a sensible idea and plan. Once they have a plan, they share it with a focus group, hoping to confirm their plan. Then they share it with those who will execute the plan. Once it is at this level, "hopeful perhaps" sounds like a formidable plan that cannot fail. Yet, it is still a "perhaps."

What am I saying? I am saying that leadership is in and of itself experimental. I know that we want to believe that our leaders fully understand what to do. There may be times that they do. Winston Churchill felt like he was prepared for his mission but each decision was based upon a practical understanding of previous wars, a calculation of current circumstances, and the hope that it would work. A "perhaps"! I am giving you permission to try and retry and "perhaps" until you find a solution for the problems and challenges that are before you—all the while hoping and believing that you are guided in your pursuit. "Perhaps" is for those who want to make a difference.

The death of creativity is predictability. Predictable success is suffocating our genius.

Success and making money is formulated so well that if you understand the process, you can duplicate it over and over. You can franchise it and it will produce money for anyone who obeys the formula. Our current social crisis needs fresh eyes and new innovative thought in order for us to find solutions to social ills that we have lived with for so long. It needs a disruption to solve a certain problem in life, business, and society. It will take creativity to cure it.

It's important to know that you can't just try to change things; you must understand the current system and why it was adopted, what problems it fixes, and what problems remain unfixed. The place where things are not fixed is the opportunity for originality. The invention is not necessarily doing something new but improving what is.

Curiosity is the key to this; curiosity about the future without curiosity about the past is ignorance. If you are a student of the current and future and you do not understand the past, then you will inevitably repeat the same mistake in the future.

John D. Rockefeller said, "If you want to succeed you should strike out on new paths, rather than travel the worn paths of accepted success."

In order to get results you never had before, you need to do what you have never done before. Society has had the same social ills for decades and many of them for centuries. Maybe your company has some problems that have gone unsolved for years. The next era needs people to do what is not expected. The father of personal development, Jim Rohn, said, "If you are not willing to risk the unusual, you will have to settle for the ordinary."

We need anointed leadership this season. We need people who know that they are anointed to solve problems and are willing to try new things, looking for new results. In my organization, we call it the Spirit to Rule. The Spirit to Rule is the spirit of an entrepreneur. The anointing of a ruler gives you the power to rule over and solve problems.

We recognize that the Spirit to Rule solves these problems:

- Poverty
- Broken-heartedness
- Captivity and imprisonment
- Lack of vision
- Oppression
- Rejection

This anointing to rule is a perfect antidote for post-modern social ills. Here is the list of postmodern ills:

- Poverty
- Drug abuse
- Imprisonment
- Violence
- Scarcity
- Domestic violence

*"A disruption in business is started in order to change the world"*
*Guy Kawasaki*

It is important that you believe that what you do is more than just making money. The only way we can change the world is to build businesses, families, nonprofits, communities, and organizations that help to change the world around us. There are many businesses that make curing the socials ills of the world a part of their business plan. As Rabbi Daniel Lapin says in his book *Business Secrets from the Bible*, "Doing business is a righteous act all by itself." By participating in the activity of business and exchange, you are making the world a better place.

Many companies not only make money and create jobs but they also pay attention to and choose to do something about the challenges of human suffering. I am not talking about handouts or giveaways. Social entrepreneurship is solving many social ills yet at the same time causing many problems. Studies have shown that when a big business gives away things to help the needy, it has crippled the local businessmen and businesswomen by taking away their customers. It's a solution but not *the* solution. Alliances will need to be formed at the local level to change the systemic issues of poverty. The only true way to deal with poverty is to empower businesses that both plant businesses and support local social and spiritual ventures. The whole man must be empowered, not merely supplied.

Empowerment is key!

The good news is that businesses are recognizing their place in changing the world. At Disney, employees have an allowance to give toward families that they encounter with special challenges. Tom's Shoes gives a pair of shoes to children in poverty for each pair sold. Dutch Bros Coffee encourages its employees to pay attention to people coming to them for their coffee. They will even take time to pray for people who appear to be struggling. A 10 Hat company plants a tree for hats that are purchased. Bill and Melinda Gates started the Gates Foundation and they are helping children around the world to have a better life. Social entrepreneurship is a growing concern for major companies. Yet, I don't believe that its only big business that should have a heart for social entrepreneurship. It starts with simply realizing that you have an anointing to bring about change and concoct cures.

We discussed being anointed for a specific assignment in a previous chapter. Let me ask how much of what you currently are doing would change if it was a divine assignment from the Creator? Let's say the Creator has anointed you to solve problems and concoct cures in your industry. Even if you are reading this and you don't believe in a Creator, what would you do to change if you could create a butterfly effect that would change the course of history in your family, business, community or country? If your contribution would disrupt something forever? The scripture says that the earth belongs to the Lord and that He has assigned higher elevations of influences to those who have the following characteristics:

- Work with innocent hands
- Have a sincere heart
- Refuse to live empty lives
- Resist gain through tricky schemes

There is a divine blessing reserved for those who choose to help others more than they choose to help themselves. If you and I use our anointing and blessing to make others lives better, then the universal laws of generosity and prosperity will help us help others.

If you are starting a business, think about what I just said. Make it bigger than making money. Make it about making history. Make it about curing someone's ills. Then you will find a purpose that can change the world and disrupt things.

Your hands and heart are an extension of you. You do with your hands what is in your heart. So, if you govern your heart, you will find that your hands will be more effective. When a person loses hope in their career, their hands work less effectively. It's like a tree. A tree grows its roots and then grows outward at its tips. Your heart is the root system and your hands are like the tips that stretch out beyond what is normal.

I know that this standard is different from common marketplace theories: to get what you want any way you want. But the next era is going to need good people to do something about the evils that are currently affecting people's lives. Your business is the staging place for good things to happen.

I encourage you to become a pioneer and entrepreneur. Become like a tree, stretch out and reach out. This will cause you to lead change.

Abraham Maslow says it this way. "With a tree, all the growth takes place at the growing tips. Humanity is exactly the same. All the growth takes place in the growing tip: among that one percent of the population. It's made up of pioneers, the beginners. That's where the action is."

That's where the action is. Submit yourself to being where the action is. The best fruit is at the tips of the branches.

I challenge you to find the tips of any industry and stretch out from that point. Concocting a cure is about finding what no one has found, solving what no one has solved, developing what no one has developed before. This doesn't mean that you start with no research or previous references. It means just the opposite. We must use what is and reach beyond it. We are not to uproot what has been, but use it as a springboard to the greater. Sheldon Gary Adelson, of Las Vegas Sands Corporation, who has $34.6 billion in net worth, said it this way: "The only way to get ahead in business is to do things differently than they are currently being done. If you do things differently success will follow you like a shadow . . . and you can't get rid of it." The fundamentals are nonnegotiable but the difference is negotiable. Business is about exchanging goods and service for compensation. It's nonnegotiable but the difference is found in how you choose to do that, what problems you choose to solve, and for whom.

We are alive in a time that affords those who are willing to be like a tree and stretch out to become very influential, impactful, and increasingly wealthy.

I look at the wealth graph yearly so that I can see if there is a change in how wealth is being distributed. In 2018 there was a shift in the distribution of wealth and an increase in the number of millionaires that moved wealth levels. The 2018 year in scope welcomed 2.3 million new millionaires, with the highest increase observed in the U.S. today. The United States is home to 43 percent of the world's millionaires. Take a look at the graph below.

You can notice a change in the poverty and middle-class platforms of the pyramid between 2016 and 2018. In addition there is a change in the $100,000 to millionaire platforms. This shift is telling me that the current economic state is a perfect ecosystem for those

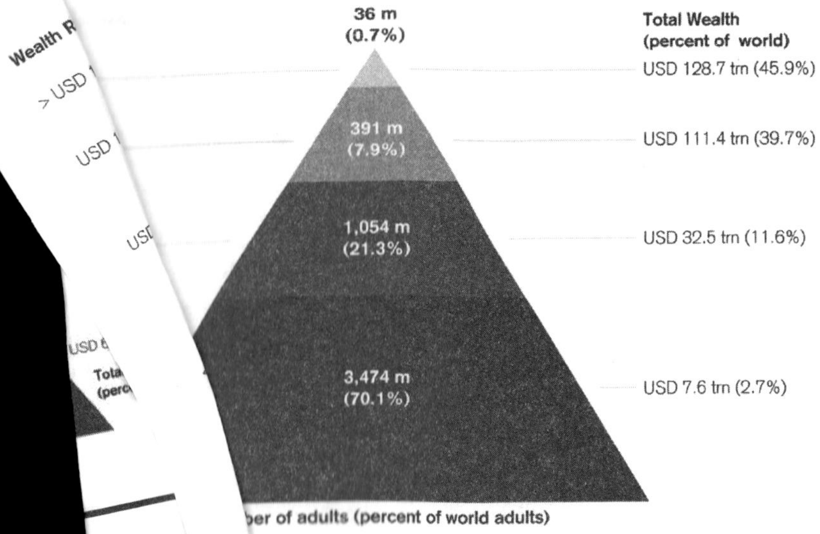


people … dle class to move up in society, if they are
lass. Thi… something different than they have ever
her peopl…
point that
n turn, fix…

… e between the pyramids, you will see a
… y and poverty to middle- and upper-mid-
…, they need … p 1 percent didn't experience any change.
… e comfortable concocting solutions that
… c security even to middle and upper-middle
is d… in g flatter each year. It's easier for someone
a… and y to make money and climb out of scarcity
… ore.

The p… more likely to come to life and have people it
helps … years ago.

It is quit… ealize that in 2018 alone there have been nearly
two and a… aires recognized. That means there was an in-
crease in k… ptitude, focus, and problem-solving that caused
2.3 million p… move from one class to another.

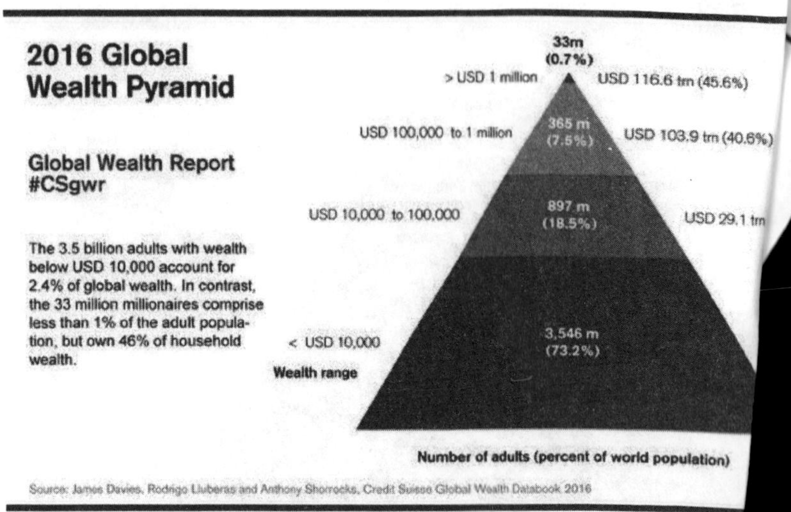


The number that is most exciting is the percentage of moved away from scarcity to the $10,000 to $100,000 exciting because they somehow developed a cure for o problems. They were able to help someone else to the fixed a problem both for them and someone else. This, their need for a financial increase.

In order for the 2.3 million millionaires to rise in statu to help cure the problems of others.

The playing field is leveling out. The only challenge what problem for which you are the solution. Second you make sure that you concoct a solution that raise those whose problems you solve?

Altruism is wonderful but we all need to live. There m both change the world and be lifted at the same time. happen for someone will in turn cause it to happen fo versal law. Have you ever tried to spray someone wit splash someone in the swimming pool? Have you noti as you spray them you also get wet?

Find a cure for someone's problem and you will also find a cure for yours. If we realize that each platform is connected to both an aptitude and a perceived need, we will be able to find solutions. By being aware of the perceived need and raising our aptitude to help solve those needs, we will find prosperity. Let's take a brief look at each of the four tiers on the platform and see what we can understand about the mindset and aptitude behind those who occupy them. We will start with the peak of the one percenters. The goal of doing this is not to tell you the keys to being a millionaire but to direct you to develop your aptitude. The greater your problem-solving skills, the greater the reward you will receive. The greater your ability to effectively execute problem-solving of other people's problems, the greater monetization you can expect.

Ascending the pyramid takes development. With each level, the demand for a different response is needed. Although the circumstance may be the same, each group in the tier levels responds to those circumstances differently. Each person's aptitude and efficacy determine the impact of the circumstance. Riches and money allow a person to respond differently. The aptitude to gain riches becomes a training ground for the next level of problems.

For instance, the economic crisis of 2008 affected each one of these wealth platforms differently. Yet each group was affected.

Abraham Maslow's pyramid of self-actualization can give us a glimpse into how each platform would function.

Maslow's self-actualization pyramid seems to correlate perfectly with the global wealth pyramid as far as perspective and aptitude are concerned.

The highest place is self-actualization and the realization of your full potential. It makes sense why the peak of the Wealth Pyramid is occupied by individuals who are entrepreneurial and leadership oriented. These individuals are comfortable with calculated risk and focus on solving larger and more global problems. Their accomplishments give them a broader scope. Their resources are people and relationships more than the amount of money they have at their disposal. They val-

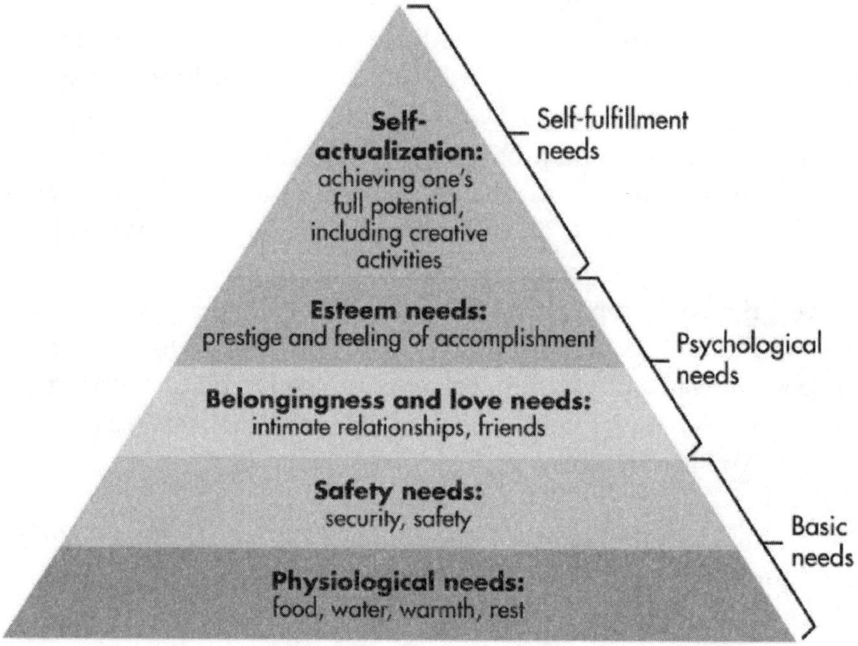


ue influence. They have to build a system of success that keeps them moving forward.

Peak-tier people's greatest need is a sense of well-being and self-fulfillment. They no longer do things for the mere need of possessing money; they seek something more.

The second levels of focus and association are different again. They are focused on their need for esteem, prestige, and the feeling of accomplishment. Their aptitude falls under psychological needs. At this level, the greatest value is predictable and formulated success, and systematic problem-solving is mainly localized with future goals for a global impact.

The psychological goals are shared by this level. The needs are different between the $10,000 to $100,000 group and the $100,000 to $1,000,000—the difference being the self-actualization needs. This group makes up just over 20 percent of the wealth distribution and they need to belong. Their greatest need is love and community. They look to make a difference to those close to them. They find and play their part on the team. They are a part of the problem-solving system. Their problem-solving most likely will be based upon moderate maintenance and minimal risk-taking on a personal level. Change is scary and only should happen if necessary.

The lowest level on the pyramid deals with those who live in scarcity. Every day they are consumed with satisfying their meager needs. Their greatest enemy is starvation. They are at risk because they live with little and have little ability to solve their basic needs. They are at risk, impoverished, and most often need help to solve their problems. Their main focus of the day is how to get their basic needs met.

They cannot move up the self-actualization pyramid because they don't have their immediate staple, which is to feel safe. If they don't have water, food, heat, or rest, they cannot feel safe. At this level, safety is not common. Their every need is about what they physically have or don't have. This platform's mindset and aptitude are directed by the basic needs of life.

These tiers of wealth and actualization are ascendable. Each individual will have to scale personally in their aptitude and environment to do so, but it is possible. That is, if the reason is powerful enough.

Every leader should be someone who desires to solve social issues. Whether that's in their organization, family, community, or in society. Leaders are anointed to concoct solutions. Every historical leader desired to do so, from Ghandi to Jesus to President Kennedy and Winston Churchill. They all desired to better the quality of life of the people whom they led. They wanted to move people up the levels of the pyramid.

Each level concocts cures to the level of their internal satisfaction. Once you have achieved and developed a processor system that helps you maintain the fundamental requirements of one level, your desire to proceed to the next will create a dissatisfaction. You will find yourself dreaming of things to try, things that will meet your needs on the next level. You will experiment with different options and opportunities to find fulfillment for your level of need. You will need to be comfortable with all of the stages of the experiment in order to understand the science of success for the level you are developing.

There are four experimentation ingredients of an alchemist:

1. *They are pioneers with an entrepreneurial mindset.* This makes them risk-takers and highly curious.
   This stage is driven by pain, pleasure, and curiosity.
   The need to achieve your goal or fulfill the need of others will cause you to pioneer new pathways. Harvey S. Firestone said, *"The way of the pioneer is always rough."*

2. *They are highly ambitious.*
   The dissatisfaction of the entrepreneur generates an ambitious desire that is subconscious and uncontrollable. It is obsessive and driven to achieve. Kim Kardashian said, *"I'm an entrepreneur. 'Ambitious' is my middle name."*

3. *They have a willingness to try and fail,* then try and fail, again and again, until they achieve their desired goal.
   Failure is not an option; failure is the way to success. Try and try again! Be driven to action! Prove your concepts! Proverbs 24:16 says, "King Solomon gives this key in his book of wisdom. He says that you must be willing to try and fall seven times."

4. *Their decisions are driven by meticulous measurements.*
   Measure and measure again is very important. The key to business in the future is high execution based upon data. We have seen the world change through this form of experimentation from Google, Facebook, etc. You must be both experimental and calculated.
   Master the fundamentals and then use experimentation to break the limit. If it's not obvious and easy to recognize maybe

it's not available because it's time for a new discovery. Mine the data and a pattern will reveal itself.

Truly, there are no limits. I watched a video of a guy in a third-world country take a stick, use it as a gardening hoe, and build a proper underground swimming pool. In America, a family would would have to pay $100,000 to construct a pool of equal size. Yet this man used his innovation and experimented with what he had until he was able to master the science of pool construction using a stick, a shoddy brick-baking oven, and local mud.

People are finding out how to get unstuck with what they have within their grasp. They use their resources and innovation to achieve whatever they can imagine. If you can imagine with deep clarity a specific lifestyle, job, business, family culture, you will discover the means to obtain it. If you have a problem, there is a solution. The fact that the problem exists is confirmation that the cure exists.

Chapter 7

# MASTERY MINDSHIFT

We have covered two of the three equations of obsession and ingredients that are necessary for the experimentalist revolution. You have discovered the art of making things happen, the strategy of breaking the common to discover the uncommon. Our final chapter will help you be the champion of change in your sphere of influence. This chapter will make you comfortable with change and instituting the change. Change is difficult when it is personal. When you know that others are counting on you, you will often experience a level of confidence that you wouldn't normally experience. When others depend on your success, you will often embrace rising to the occasion. This can alleviate some of the pain associated with making something happen. The altruistic side of us is willing to do whatever it takes to better humanity, to better others' lives. Yet, the bigger picture is often shrouded by an imaginary picture that the grass is greener on the other side. The grass-is-greener syndrome has caused many to miss their best and greatest opportunities.

There was such a man who was a farmer in South Africa. He loved farming but wasn't able to produce what he needed to keep the farm running properly.

Although he loved having a farm, he didn't enjoy the hardships that befell him in keeping up the farm. Flooding, drought, and pestilence overwhelmed him. He heard that many people were striking it rich through mining diamonds. He decided to sell his farm and set out on a journey to discover his fortune in diamonds. After a season of searching, the man was very frustrated and discouraged with his pursuit. He had spent all of his money and emotional energy. He was at his end and threw himself in a river and died. Meanwhile, on his old farm, the new owner was walking the land and noticed a strange black rock about the size of a grapefruit. He picked it up, took it home, and placed it on his mantlepiece. One day a close friend was visiting and saw the rock. He asked the farmer if he knew what it was. The farmer responded, "It's a quartz rock." The friend quickly retorted with, "It's a diamond!" The farmer said, "This is unbelievable! There are acres and acres of these stones all over my property!" His farm became one of the richest diamond producers in the world. The old farmer sold his farm and lost his life looking for something that was right in front of him.

This story is from *Acres of Diamonds* by Russell H. Conwell. The first farmer loved the land and farming but didn't like the challenges of flooding, pests, etc., all the challenges that come with being a farmer. Sometimes we like doing something but not being something. He liked farming but didn't like being a farmer. What you choose to do and choose to become are determined by something more than your talent, skill, or ability. More often it is determined by our emotional wealth and health, which is made up of three factors: IQ, EQ, and AQ, which can be simplistically defined as follows:

- IQ, or Intelligence Quotient: the intelligence, knowledge, facts, and trivia that one possesses
- EQ, or Emotional Quotient: the emotional understanding and capability of self and others that help with different situations and people
- AQ, or Adaptability Quotient: the ability to adapt to and thrive in an environment of change

Each of these is equally important in the making of a champion of change, but most of this conversation will be around AQ. It was the farmer's AQ level that caused him not to be able to adapt to becoming a farmer even though he loved farming. A farmer needs to love solving the problems of flooding, pestilence, and all of the other issues that the second farmer endured until he became a farmer of diamonds, which I am sure brought about a whole load of challenges of its own.

In the same way, self-actualization levels must be mastered before a person can ascend to the next level. I believe that increasing your IQ and EQ will only benefit your AQ.

Please keep in mind that my goal in addressing the concepts of IQ, EQ, and AQ is not exhaustive research. I hope to simply shed a little light on the subject and allow you, the reader, to dive deeper into the subject through your own personal research. My hope is to tie a tidy little string to all of these concepts, leaving you with a vivid enough picture to pay attention to their effects on your pattern for achievement and success.

## IQ: THE INTELLIGENCE, KNOWLEDGE, FACTS, AND TRIVIA THAT ONE POSSESSES

A few years ago I served on a coalition that served one of the needy areas in Seattle. One of the conversations was around IQ. The questions were whether or not the IQ test was relevant for every ethnic and economic status. Should there be an IQ test for specific economic levels?

We never came to any concrete answer. I believe the reason was that the objective of the IQ test was not clarified nor was the objective of changing clarified.

Is it about general knowledge or is it about conclusion?

I know lots of people who have a lot of general knowledge and have very high IQs but they can't practically solve a problem. Is the objective of an IQ test to show how much knowledge you have collected? Or is it about having the knowledge necessary to solve the issues of your sphere of influence. I know people who would do an amazing job on *Who Wants to Be a Millionaire* but are hardly enterprising in life. I really enjoyed the movie *Slumdog Millionaire.* The young man in the film gained knowledge for his circumstance through his life experiences and won the game. People learn in many different ways. I believe the separation is not how you learn but that you learn, that you become proficient in how to best use what you learn to benefit your quality of life and the lives of those around you.

All I know is for a purpose and for use. This is what makes the difference between someone who can play *Jeopardy* and someone who can make millions or start a nonprofit organization that changes lives. The knowledge must be pragmatic.

The farmer's lack of intelligence in how to identify a diamond caused him to walk past a fortune every day of his life. Even as he searched the earth for the precious gems, he never considered that those odd quartz rocks on his farm could have been diamonds. He didn't know what to do with the information that he gathered.

I am not sure how to test this level of general knowledge, but I do know that focusing on learning from every circumstance and becoming a lifetime learner through books, mentors, coaches, training, and life-experiences will grow your IQ and your ability to recognize patterns and shapes. This is what I believe the first IQ test really is.

Have you ever seen a baby take a square shape and try to plug it into a round hole? The first few times they will try to force it, slam it, yell at it, and even throw it in frustration. But after a few times of being shown how the patterns and shapes work together, they have the ability to match the shapes and patterns. This is true for us as adults. When faced with a challenge, we may respond the same as a baby. We try to force it, slam it, yell at it, and throw it in frustration. But our determination will not allow us to stop there, so we collect more information until we understand the shape and the pattern. From this point, we will never have a challenge with that problem again. We know how it all works.

I once watched a documentary about Warren Buffet. It didn't take me long to understand how he could be so skilled in one area and inept in another. It's what he gives his intelligence to. He spends most of his day, 8-10 hours, reading the *Wall Street Journal* and other business-informing periodicals. His mental capacity along with his appetite for knowledge in this area allow him to see shapes and patterns in the market before others. I am not sure what his general knowledge IQ score is, but if you give him an IQ test around his specialized knowledge he would be the Einstein of this century in business. He easily extrapolates and uses knowledge from trends and previous patterns and can see how things most likely will unfold in the future.

Increase your IQ by becoming like a child. Be curious every day. Ask lots of questions. Discover new things daily. See how this thing fits with that thing. Be a lifetime learner and the IQ, intelligence, knowledge, facts, and trivia that you possess will top the charts, preparing you to grow emotionally.

## EQ

The farmer became a diamond chaser because he was emotionally ignorant of how to maintain joy under the pressure of farming. His lack of EI caused him to chase a dream and ultimately surrender to the emotion of sorrow, which caused him to throw himself into the river and take his life.

Once the child from our earlier illustration learns how to match the shapes and colors, he gains a greater level of emotional control. The child learns how to relate the square peg with the square hole and the round peg with the round hole. The more he does it, the more joy he gets. The more he gets our attention, the more he wants to do it. He is known to engage the world around him with a greater level of emotional intelligence from an increase of his intelligence quotient. The more life a person experiences affords them the power to interpret circumstances differently.

Again, back to Warren Buffet. I am not sure what kind of economic crisis would cause him to lose emotional confidence, but I am sure that it's a different level of downturn that very few markets have seen. Why? Because he has experienced downturns in the market, has been educated through them, and has learned strategies and tools from them, thus giving him a greater efficacy of how to handle them. He doesn't need to lose his emotional well-being for financial markets because he is intelligent about them.

There are several schools of thought around what emotional intelligence is, but I have found four common places of agreement, most being that emotional intelligence covers self-awareness, self-regulation, social awareness, and relationship regulation.

Daniel Goleman, author of the book *Emotional Intelligence,* offers this insight: "If your emotional abilities aren't in hand, if you don't have self-awareness, if you are not able to manage your distressing emotions, if you can't have empathy and have effective relationships, then no matter how smart you are, you are not going to get very far." No matter where you research, you will find something along those lines. The wiki pages on EI list these same four ideas as emotional abilities (https:// en.m.wikipedia.org/wiki/Emotional_intelligence):

1. Perceiving emotions—the ability to detect and decipher emotions in faces, pictures, voices, and cultural artifacts—including the ability to identify one's own emotions. Perceiving emotions represents a basic aspect of emotional intelligence, as it makes all other processing of emotional information possible. This is called Self-Awareness—the ability to recognize your emotions and know your strengths and limits.

2. Using emotions—the ability to harness emotions to facilitate various cognitive activities, such as thinking and problem-solving. The emotionally intelligent person can capitalize fully upon his or her changing moods in order to best fit the task at hand. This is considered Self-Regulation—the ability to choose how we think, how we feel, and the actions we take.

3. Understanding emotions—the ability to comprehend emotional language and to appreciate complicated relationships among emotions. For example, understanding emotions encompasses the ability to be sensitive to slight variations between emotions, and the ability to recognize and describe how emotions evolve over time. This is Social Awareness—the ability to understand and respond to the needs of others. Empathy.

4. Managing emotions—the ability to regulate emotions in both ourselves and in others. Therefore, the emotionally intelligent person can harness emotions, even negative ones, and manage them to achieve intended goals. This is Relationship Management—the ability to inspire and influence others and sort out the conflicts that arise.

Daniel Goleman adds motivation to the list. "Our emotional intelligence determines our potential for learning the practical skills that are based on its five elements: self-awareness, motivation, self-regulation, empathy, and adeptness in relationships."

Whether motivation should be listed or not I believe that we can all agree that emotional intelligence is a needed skill set to develop. We all should be aware of ourselves, aware of our abilities and inabilities. Otherwise, our ability to be effective on a team, in a family, or in society is hindered. We all should be aware of our ability to choose and decipher how we feel and what to do with our emotions.

This is not talent; it's a development. Just like most things that we have discussed in this book, one path leads to the next. If you don't seek to understand yourself and your ability, or lack thereof, you will not be able to understand how to regulate yourself. If we think back to the shape development of the child, she was in a state of learning and regulating. If a person cannot regulate themselves, they will find it difficult, maybe impossible, to have empathy for the world around them. How many times do you need to be cut off in a grocery store by someone who is completely oblivious of you to realize that we need more people aware of the world around them? We need a world with more empathy in order to make it run smoothly. We can all agree that relationships can be difficult at times. Building solid relationships is complicated, but if we all grew in the first three abilities of EI this would definitely be easier. Learning how to regulate relationships is something that we have been doing all of our lives.

As children we get excited when our parents celebrate our success. For instance, a child learning to walk will try again and again even though she falls, because a parent claps and rejoices over her efforts. So, she keeps doing it over and over just to get another response from her parent.

Take a moment and think back to the first farmer. What level of emotional intelligence did he falter in? We know that he faltered because he threw himself in the river and drowned. At some point his emotional intelligence ran out and he was not able to adapt to his position in life. This is a tragic end for anyone because an alchemist always has one more recipe to attempt. Was it because he didn't have the proper level of ego? Did he lack the self-awareness to regulate himself? He didn't know how to regulate the obsession and keep his emotion in check. Or was it because his chase for diamonds was bigger than why he was chasing diamonds? Did he not have anyone he was empathizing with? Did he not know that he lived in a world that needed him to help it become better? Was his world completely about him and not a greater good that he was anointed for? Suicide is a desperate response to hitting a wall, a wall that can be shifted with AQ.

## AQ, OR ADAPTABILITY QUOTIENT: THE ABILITY TO ADAPT TO AND THRIVE IN AN ENVIRONMENT OF CHANGE

Remember, Thomas Edison said, "To invent you need a good imagination and a pile of junk."

We must possess the knowledge base, the emotional fortitude, to frequently rise to the challenges that present themselves. Without confidence in these areas, it is nearly impossible to possess the adaptability that can bring about change.

Winston Churchill possessed knowledge both from experience and history, as well as the emotional intelligence to handle the moment at hand, which, in turn, gave him the adaptability. If you follow his career in handling Hitler and the Nazis, you can see the full functionality of adaptability. No battle was executed perfectly, but through adaptability the victory was secured.

This is not about settling into mediocrity. This is about mastery of the circumstances. IQ is mastery of the data. EQ is mastery of the mind, will, and emotions. AQ is mastery of your destiny. Circumstances don't have the right to master your destiny. You have to master the circumstances and resources to master your destiny. There is often a proving ground before you ascend to the next level.

It would be easy to say that the second farmer in the *Acres of Diamonds* story had it easier than the first. The realization is that he bought the farm (that sounds like a familiar phrase). In buying the farm came the love for the dirt and for farming but the floods, the pests, and the droughts also came with the purchase. Yet, he didn't allow those challenges to deter him. He endured until he was presented with an opportunity to adapt. He went from being a farmer to being a diamond miner. Yes, I believe the transition from farming to diamond mining would have been an easier transition but it still would have its challenges. He would have to develop his IQ and EQ in order to continue to develop his AQ into a diamond miner. If he never had that wilderness experience, he wouldn't have had a reason to adapt and change. If he didn't change, he couldn't change his circumstances.

Napoleon Hill, in his book *Outwitting the Devil*, talks about a conversation with the personification of fear, doubt, and worry just before he published the book *Think and Grow Rich*. He had to confront his devils in order to become the world teacher of the 17 principles of success. Adaptability is discovered when you confront the devil or the monster in your story.

You can recognize him because he always doubts who you are and your abilities. The scripture speaks of such a moment with the Teacher. The devil's voice speaks to him in the wilderness: "If You are the Son of God, tell this stone to become bread."

If you have faced your devils, this statement of doubt and challenge, designed to bring about fear, would sound or feel familiar. You may be looking doubt in the face right now. The very statement is important to lock in on. The night doesn't really know who you are. The ghost in the darkness doesn't really have a grasp on your potential. Fear, doubt, and worry speak from uncertainty and unclear dimensions. They are hoping that you don't know yourself either.

This is where adaptability comes in. You may not be exactly who you want to be, but you have the efficacy to keep learning, growing, and changing until you become that person. This is frightening to the unknown. The unknown wants you to give up and never embrace your potential. No one will ever know if you could have become what you hoped for, what you dreamed of, and what you were destined to become. Adaptability won't allow you to be afraid, worried, or doubtful to the level of quitting.

The other thought about the devil's challenge to the Teacher is that he does understand one thing clearly: that humanity has the potential to turn a rock into bread. The devil's perspective of the human potential risk as God's children is limitless. He didn't understand that he was unlocking the Nazarene's potential with this challenge. The Nazarene was going from a carpenter to the Anointed One through this test. His AQ would not embrace the fear, the worry, or doubt. He wouldn't allow the thought of inadequacy to hinder his opportunity to change and become the champion of change.

If you can change, you can make change happen. If you can grow, you can make growth happen.

The devil's challenge to the Teacher demanded a response, which was, "It is written, 'Man shall not live on bread alone.'" Bread is never enough for a person who has an objective. God has placed the anointed on the earth for a reason, and it isn't to eat bread. God has anointed you for a reason, and it's not just to eat bread and have temporary satisfaction. There is a bigger picture for your life. The devil will always try to get you to think about the temporary. Fear, doubt, and worry will always talk about momentary issues.

I remember the fear that embraced me when I first started the journey of success. I was afraid of everything. I would lie in bed all morning because I was afraid to make the phone calls that I needed to make. I was reading the book *Who Moved My Cheese* and started asking one single question: What would I do if I wasn't afraid? Once that thought came across my mind, I would jump out of bed quickly before the next thought—*It won't work*—could reveal itself.

I developed my AQ by instituting a simple ritual of asking myself the question, "What would you do if you weren't afraid?" It was easy to say "It won't work," but I needed to have something to say to override the stopping statement and move toward the objective. The Teacher used scripture from the Bible as His starting statement. I used a statement from the book *Who Moved My Cheese.* You don't have to be original with the statement, just make sure that it empowers you to go and not stop running until you have accomplished the goal. Use this strategy to overcome procrastination and hesitation—these are distractions from your destiny.

You can have an anointing to bring about change, but hesitation and procrastination will steal your destiny. You can be the answer but if you don't show up, the problem goes unsolved. That's why AQ is necessary. You must believe that you can change, that you are the change that must take place, and that you can change whatever challenge reveals itself. You are anointed for your company, family, and community to bring about change. You are the alchemist who is anointed to help find a cure. You are anointed to harness things to bring about health, life, and prosperity. The anointing gives you the power and authority over all material things, converting it to spiritual and spiritual to material. The alchemist harnesses the material available to bring about cures and prosperity.

The second farmer saw and seized his opportunity once he recognized the potential. In the book *The Oz Principle*, there is a principle for moving forward into AQ:

1. See It. Acknowledge change is needed
2. Own It. Take ownership of the situation.
3. Solve It. Develop an action plan asking one question, "What else can I (we) do?"
4. Do It. Execute the change.

Andy Grove, from Intel, said this about seeing and seizing the moment: "Every company faces a critical point when it must change dramatically to rise to the next level of performance. If the company fails to see and seize that moment, it will start to decline. The key is courage."

The separation between those who strike when it's hot and those who miss the moment is courage.

The definition of courage is exactly what you would think it would be. There are no surprises in its definition. One of my favorite resources is Noah Webster's Dictionary of 1828. His definitions are slightly richer than our modern version. According to the 1828 dictionary, "Courage is that quality of mind which enables men to encounter danger and difficulties with firmness, or without fear or depression of spirits." It is very rich, isn't it? Courage is a mental capacity that refuses to allow danger or difficulties to deter you from a firm stance. Courage is necessary for any level of success.

Winston Churchill said, "Success is not final, failure is not fatal: it is the courage to continue that counts."

Courage is somewhat mysterious. Some speak of courage as if it needs to be stirred up and produced. Some think of it as just a part of a personality type. What if courage is a by-product of something? Let's say, an obsession. I find that people who have courage are obsessed with something to the degree that they are not concerned with the challenges or dangers associated with it.

Let's alchemize this thought. IQ and EQ give way to AQ, of which the active ingredient is courage. The fast track to courage is to be obsessed with something. Obsessed people are constantly challenging their understanding of the object that captured their attention. They can't collect enough information. The more they know, the more emotional they get about the subject. The more they get emotionally involved, the more courage they have to invest into the pursuit of the subject. In the book *The Alchemist*, by Paulo Coelho, there is a boy taking a journey. When he started the journey, he was simple in his knowledge and emotional connectivity to the world. The more he journeyed, the more he learned. The more he learned, the more emotionally astute he became. Each day brought about new things and new challenges. As he traveled he learned about how to read omens.

Something that he never knew before the experience made him even more determined to achieve his goal. One day he saw a vision of war and realized that the people whom he was visiting were in danger. He shared the dream and found out that it was a dangerous thing to share omens. It led to him having a sword's tip at his forehead. The man holding the sword asked a series of questions, then he withdrew the sword and said, "I had to test your courage . . . Courage is the quality most essential to understanding the language of the world."

The boy's obsession turned him into someone who was willing to give his life to save others. This is something that he didn't possess before something possessed him. He was possessed with finding his "personal legend," which is what *The Alchemist* calls finding your destiny. He became so enthusiastic about what he was doing that he was possessed with the subject. Courage and enthusiasm work together as by-products of being obsessed. "Enthusiasm" comes from the Latin word *entheo*, which means "prophetic ecstasy, to be possessed by God."

Enthusiasm and courage begin to manifest as you are possessed with God's passion for something. The whole earth begins to speak the language of your obsession. Your sight begins to notice anything associated with it. You have the ability to see clearly past the challenges as if they were never there.

When I was in high school I took a speech class. I didn't really know why I chose to speak. As the class went on, it was clear that I would have to prepare a speech to share in front of the class. There were about thirty kids in the class. On the day that I was scheduled to give my speech, I skipped class. I was so frightened to stand in front of people and speak. It wasn't that I didn't like people looking at me, because I was the class clown. But there was something different about standing in front of people and giving a speech.

Fast forward a few years later. I was invited into a network marketing business that I was very excited about. It took over my thoughts and emotions. I loved the idea of being in business, helping people, and making big money. Lots of money. The more the better. I connected the business with my dream lifestyle. One day I needed to schedule a meeting to propose this business opportunity to a group of people about the same size room as my speech class. I took my place and shared the business opportunity and never once experienced fright. I was cured! Yes! I was possessed with the possibility of living out my dream. I was obsessed with the notion of being wealthy to the point that I didn't care what people thought anymore. The courage to speak wasn't the issue. I had chosen to be possessed by my obsession. My enthusiasm made my actions look courageous, but in reality, I was possessed by God's dream for my life. When you are possessed with God's dream, you become obsessed with it. Every alchemist is possessed with a God-sized dream.

This God-sized dream will build within you so much enthusiasm and courage that you will despise anything that would try to shamefully stop you. You will become so passionate that you will persist beyond anything that could embarrass you. A God-sized dream is like a carrot dangling in front of a horse. It becomes the joy set before you that makes you shameless in your pursuit of that dream. Living possessed by a God-sized dream is the obsession of an alchemist.

I believe that Walt Disney was right when he said, "All our dreams can come true if we have the courage to pursue them." Walt Disney himself was possessed with a God-sized dream. Many would say that he was obsessed with his magical dream. Courage is easy for someone who is possessed with a dream bigger than themselves. The dream is too big to get stuck on thinking about themselves.

Your ability to adapt to changing and challenging circumstances will be increased by a God-sized dream that you become obsessed with. The development of a healthy ego is found in the God-sized dream. It's what makes you persist when others give up.

One day a certain man received communication that a really good friend of his was going to stop over. It was customary that he would be ready for visitors to stop by on a Friday evening and stay the weekend. But his friend's coming seemed to have caught him at an inconvenient time. How would he prepare for his friend who would arrive at any moment? It was in the early morning hour that he thought, *Where could I get bread and wine at this hour?* He remembered that his neighbor was always borrowing things from him. He decided to call on him. He ran next door and knocked softly. There was no answer. He then knocked a little bit harder. Still, no answer. Then he began to pound on the door. Then he heard someone calling from inside, "Who is it?"

"It is your neighbor. I need to borrow some bread. I have a friend coming and I don't have anything to prepare for him."

The neighbor's response was, "Go away! We are all sleeping."

He knocked again with more force and said, "Please give me some bread for my visitor!"

The neighbor said, "Go away! We are all in bed and I will not open the door and give you bread."

Then he knocked even louder and yelled more forcefully, "I need you to give me bread!"

The neighbor finally opened the door and gave the man bread, saying, "Here, I am giving you this because of your persistence."

The man returned home and welcomed his friend. This story is originally told in the Greek language. In Greek, the word "persistence" and the word "shamelessness" are the same.

## SHAME THRESHOLD

We must be so possessed with our goal that it generates courage and shamelessness that persist beyond the obstacles.

Shame and the fear of shame are the reason many people never achieve their goals and find their "personal legends."

Virginia Sturm, a postdoctoral fellow at the Memory and Aging Center of the University of California, San Francisco, reported at the American Academy of Neurology annual meeting that the Cingulate Cortex part of the brain can regulate how much, or little, you experience shame. Shame is not just an emotion or a feeling; it is also physical. She says, "Feelings like guilt, pride, shame, and embarrassment all tend to occur in the presence of others, and result largely from how we think others perceive us." "The smaller the CC region," she says, "the less embarrassed people were."

Yet, that data doesn't mean that you can't develop a level of shamelessness needed to achieve what you always wanted. The pursuit is really based on hunger. Hunger is the product of not being satisfied.

A persistent person has a predetermined image that they are moving toward. This is the part of the brain that I want to talk about. It's not the place of shamelessness, but it the area of the brain that controls the dream, destiny, God-sized dream, and personal legend. This area of the brain is called your Reticular Activating System (RAS).

The internal imagery that you feed your mind through words and pictures causes an emotional reflex that gets you moving toward finding a solution. This is again that process of IQ + EQ = AQ. Your intelligence is not just information and data; it's imagery as well. Your imagery works for you to create the fuel for the dream in the form of courage, enthusiasm, and persistence.

When you feed your mind the right information, it goes to work to bring about a solution. If you don't feed your mind the right information, your emotional intelligence will cause stress rather than confidence and you will be overwhelmed without the mental capacity to make the right choices. At this point, you will be drawn to ease and familiarity as a solution rather than looking for new ones.

When feeding your mind the right information in the form of both words and pictures, your RAS begins to filter out unusable information, only allowing information that is associated with the dream and goals. This is what is happening when you start to notice things that pertain to your goal. Things come into view that you didn't spot before. Your eyes start to look for things that relate to and help you reach the goal of the internal image. If you don't see it in your life, it will create frustration. You start to experience cognitive dissonance, which basically describes the tension of attempting to hold two opposing thoughts in your mind. This tension must be persisted through.

At this point, you will feel shame for not being where you imagined you would be by now. You can always recognize when shame is trying to get you to sabotage your persistence opportunity. Your body gets flooded with cortisol as your adrenal glands are activated by conflict in the brain. Your eyes start to look down or away. Your face starts to feel warm as you begin to blush. Your physical posture drops and your shoulders slump. Your heart begins to race as the adrenal glands release more cortisol. This causes your major arteries to constrict, raising the heart rate, and pushes glucose into your muscles. This process is a layman's description of what happens physically when you start to feel stressed. If not handled properly, it will kick you into a flight-or-fight reflex that keeps you from your dreams.

The way to wake up out of this glucose-induced coma is to create a picture that makes you want to fight rather than flee. Persistence is the same as shamelessness. You will have to set joy in your future. Establish a mental image of you, in the future, that feeds your mind the energy necessary to push past anything. You will feel the desire to slide backward but you will have to remember why you want this image. My suggestion is that the dream shouldn't only include you. You should have someone for whom you are fighting to create empathy. You can't both feel sorry for yourself and empathetic at the same time. Tap into empathy and defuse shame.

Empathy is a tool that makes the dream bigger than yourself. Decide that you want to make money for more than the big car, vacations, and the big house. After you have those things, what's the driving motivation? Feeding the poor? Making jobs for others? A better quality of life for your family? Yes, we all should want the thrill of the chase, but we should also find a way to tap into empathy and compassion for others. This has been proven to disable shame rather than being disabled by shame.

Generate a goal-oriented life that activates the RAS. This will enable you to see the goal so clearly that you can see your role. If you can see the role, you can become the role player—like an actor who reads a screen play. They see themselves in the role so clearly that it becomes their real self. Feed your mind the right pictures and words until you become the role, at which point the goals become a set of benchmarks on the way to your becoming that part.

Ernest Hemingway said, "Courage is grace under pressure." What do you look like when you are under pressure? Courage is when you keep the same poise through the pressure as you had before the pressure began. The reason your goal must become a role is the difference between who you are and who you desire to be. This will be the starting point of the pressure. The pressure will increase and test your resolve toward the goal. If you lose the poise or grace that you started with, you will have failed the test to be who you have set a goal to become.

Keep the image and role in your mind and fight for it until you become it. At this point you will no longer have to fight for it but you will have accomplished it. Your grace, the call, and destiny to become what you envision empower you to move forward no matter what the challenge might be. This is what Winston Churchill was talking about when he said that he felt as if he were "walking with destiny." He was no longer separate from his destiny, looking at it from the outside. He was now one with his destiny; he was completely in the role and was functioning in what he had always imagined. You, too, if you have not already, will find yourself looking at life from within your destiny.

At this point, everything that you have experienced in life will begin to work together for the good. You will find yourself one with your Creator and your call. You will have discovered His purpose for you and the very reason you exist. The world will become your oyster and the fruit of your destiny its pearl. It will seem as if everything is made to help you become and do what you are called to do.
Anything that resists your call will become usable material for the pearl to form.

In *The Alchemist*, the boy found his treasure in the chapel where his journey started. The purpose of the journey was to develop and hone his ability to learn to listen to the soul of the world and understand the language of the world.

In this place, you must stand your ground in the grace that is yours. You must despise shame as if it were mud on your shoes. You do not have the time or convenience of shrinking back; you must persist. Winston Churchill's voice rings in your ears: "Never retreat! Never surrender!"

At this point you will be one with the universe and God will have begun to fulfill the dream. Your ego will have connected with the greatest ego of all. God dreams big and now you have joined His big dream. You cannot look into the face and mind of God and be a small thinker. Give yourself to your walk with destiny. Give yourself to your God-sized dream. Don't talk your ego down. Lift it to match who God sees you to be.

When shame raises its ugly head, you must respond like a boxer and blacken its eye. As I mentioned before, I grew up in a house with Golden Glove champions and a three-time Olympic boxer. I also grew up as the only black kid in the school. Fighting was the only option. Today you have an enemy to your destiny. It's like gravity: you must fight for every inch that you want. Wear down your enemy and deliver the knockout blow once you see his guard drop. Resistance doesn't give up; persistence overpowers it.

You are destined to do the impossible. You are designed to harness the impossible. Let's read Winston Churchill's quote one more time: "I felt as if I were walking with destiny, and that all my past life had been but a preparation for this hour and for this trial . . . I thought I knew a good deal about it all, I was sure I should not fail." *He was sure he should not fail.* That's the confidence that I want you to have. That's a dynamic AQ: the understanding that you can adapt to whatever is next and that you will not fail, no matter what tomorrow brings. Winston Churchill had been resisted and challenged so often in life that he knew the power of getting up and trying again.

Destiny makes sure that what you have gone through will guarantee your victory. You will not fail if you have courage. Courage under pressure forces your mind to find the solutions. It may appear to some that both farmers had courage. That's true at face value, but it takes more courage to stand and fight than it does to flee. Sometimes the fight is the purpose. Once you win, all of the people watching will have the courage to fight also. Fight the good fight of faith and win the prized run as a winner. Live like a champion. Become obsessed with your purpose and it will fuel your ego with courage and persistence.

John F. Kennedy said, "Effort and courage are not enough without purpose and direction." Effort and courage need something to pursue. In order for you to possess courage, you must have a big enough vision that demands it. Courage fuels the ability to manifest change in any circumstance. Adaptability is not only about your ability to adapt to circumstances but also your ability to make circumstances adapt to you and your purpose.

My second favorite book in the world is *Green Eggs and Ham* by Doctor Seuss—second only to the Bible. I have done leadership and sales trainings based upon the great wisdom found within its pages. If you have never read it, you must. It's a beautiful picture of persistence, shamelessness, and courage. Sam is offering free breakfast to a gentleman reading a paper. The gentleman makes it very clear that he doesn't want green eggs and ham. Sam asks the man, "Do you like green eggs and ham?" The man says emphatically, "No! I do not like green eggs and ham!" Sam continues, "Would you like them here or there?" The man says, "I would not like them here or there, I would not like them anywhere." That's when most people would quit. But not Sam. Sam continues, "Would you like them in a house, with a mouse?" You can guess what the man's response would be. Sam continues and continues and continues until the man is willing to try the green eggs and ham.

I can't tell you the whole story because of copyright, but ultimately he declares that he likes green eggs and ham. Sam was walking with destiny and became one with his destiny without changing his message. He change the method of delivering the message, but he never changed his offering. Each time he changed the plan, he had enough courage to try it. When that plan didn't work, he didn't give up; he changed the method and tried again. When that didn't work, he tried again and again and again.

The experimentalist revolution is about permission to be like Sam. Try, try, and try again until you have the results you are looking for. It's hard to try again if you don't change the method. Don't be like the first farmer who decided to change the message before he tried a few more things to work the farm. Perhaps if he had stayed a little bit longer on the farm and persisted through a few more floods and challenges, destiny would have revealed to him what the strange-looking quartz stones all around were.

If you have come this far into the book without stopping, then you have persisted beyond the parts that didn't interest you, beyond the parts that didn't speak to you, to reach this point, the last page. I believe that gives me the right as your coach, mentor, or pastor to say, *Go for it!* You have what it takes to make it happen.

Harness everything! Take the pile of junk and make something amazing! Let obsession fuel a healthy ego until you accomplish everything that you dream of. Dream God-sized dreams! Be romantic. You can change the world around you and even the whole world if you dream of such a thing. This world is your inheritance, so do something with it. Leave it better than it was when you came. You brought something to this world with you that will make it better. Use it.

Don't hold back. Go full on! Give your all and leave nothing on the table. Experience success and take a wise risk. Love hard and love big. Look into the face of God as you fly at God levels. You are an *experimentalist*! Never retreat! Never surrender!